Rhetorical Philosophy and Theory
Series Editor, David Blakesley

Other Books in the Rhetorical Philosophy and Theory Series

Gorgias and the New Sophistic Rhetoric

Gorgias

and the

New Sophistic Rhetoric

Bruce McComiskey

Southern Illinois University Press
Carbondale and Edwardsville

Library of Congress Cataloging-in-Publication Data

McComiskey, Bruce, 1963–
     Gorgias and the new sophistic rhetoric / Bruce McComiskey.
          p. cm. — (Rhetorical philosophy and theory)
     Includes bibliographical references and index.
     1. Plato. Gorgias. 2. Rhetoric, Ancient. 3. Gorgias, of
     Leontini. 4. Sophists (Greek philosophy) I. Title. II. Series.

PA4279.G7 M38 2002
808'.00938—dc21
ISBN 0-8093-2397-4 (cloth : alk. paper)   00-068763

For Karen, Scott, Jonathan, and Stephen Pickard

The first case for sophistry, then, is an historical and scholarly one: that there is in sophistry a field worth studying, and a fertility in that field, constantly productive of new "sophistries," worth understanding.

—Roger Moss

Contents

Acknowledgments

The revival of classical rhetoric in communication studies and English departments across the country has sparked renewed interest in a number of historical figures, not the least of whom are the sophists, and this book would not exist, of course, without the dedicated and careful scholarship of those who believe that the sophists have something important to say to contemporary scholars of rhetoric. Earlier works by Sharon Crowley, Richard Enos, Susan Jarratt, Jasper Neel, John Poulakos, Takis Poulakos, Edward Schiappa, and Victor Vitanza, among many others, have cleared the ground for *Gorgias and the New Sophistic Rhetoric*.

This book grew out of generative debates I have had over the years with a number of people, especially Janice Lauer, Ed Schiappa, and Jim Berlin, and it is to them, as always, that I am most grateful. I would also like to thank John Stevens, whose help with translating Gorgias's *Encomium of Helen* was invaluable.

Gorgias and the New Sophistic Rhetoric is dedicated to my sister, Karen, my brother-in-law, Scott, and my nephews, Jonathan and Stephen, who may not agree with its historical approach but whose love and support make everything possible.

Portions of this book have appeared elsewhere. Chapters 1 and 2 are derived largely, with some revisions, from "Disassembling Plato's Critique of Rhetoric in the *Gorgias*" (*Rhetoric Review* 11 [1992]: 79–90; reprinted with the permission of Lawrence Erlbaum) and "Gorgias and the Art of Rhetoric: A Holistic Reading of the Extant Gorgianic Fragments" (*Rhetoric Society Quarterly* 27 [1997]: 5–24). Chapter 5 is a greatly expanded version of "The Global Village, Multiculturalism, and the Functions of Sophistic Rhetoric" (*Rhetoric, the Polis, and the Global Village*. Ed. C. Jan Swearingen. Mahwah, NJ: Lawrence Erlbaum, 1999. 75–82; reprinted with the permission of Lawrence Erlbaum). Finally, some of the sources listed in the appendix appeared originally in "Sophistic Rhetoric and Philosophy: A Selective Bibliography of Scholarship in English since 1900" (*Rhetoric Society Quarterly* 24 [1994]: 25–38).

Gorgias and the New Sophistic Rhetoric

Introduction

Throughout the 1970s and 1980s, scholars in the humanities witnessed a revival of sophistic doctrines and many "neosophistic" applications of these doctrines to contemporary disciplines. But throughout the 1990s, some important developments occurred: we learned a great deal more about the sophists as individual thinkers, creating a new need to reassess our understanding of this disparate group of traveling teachers, and some important critiques of neosophistic appropriations have given rise to new opportunities to rethink the contribution of ancient sophistic doctrines to contemporary pedagogical and political ends. In *Gorgias and the New Sophistic Rhetoric,* I examine the sophistic revival and its recent correctives specifically in relation to rhetorical studies.

The Sophists

Who were the sophists? This question is more difficult to answer than most people realize. There is evidence that *any* wise person in the ancient Greek world was called a sophist, yet we learn from some twentieth-century scholarship on fifth-century BCE Greek oratory that the sophists held certain beliefs in common, yet (again) when we read the extant texts of the sophists, we see radical differences among them, from their uses of style to their epistemological beliefs and political commitments.

The question "Who were the sophists?" was difficult to answer even for authors who lived and studied from classical antiquity into late antiquity. Plato's influence on the negative usage of the term sophist was so potent that Aristotle, and many rhetoricians yet to come, would only use the term in reference to the most unethical speakers of their day. Following are just a few voices from the Platonic corpus that characterize Plato's view of the sophists:

1

Stranger: [the sophist's] art may be traced as a branch of the appropriative, acquisitive family . . . which hunts man, privately, for hire, taking money in exchange, having the semblance of education—and this is termed Sophistry, and is the hunt after young men of wealth and rank. (*Sophist* 223b)

Stranger: The upshot is, then, the Sophist possesses a sort of reputed and apparent knowledge on all subjects, but not the reality. (*Sophist* 233c)

Anytus: I hope no relative of mine or any of my friends, Athenian or foreign, would be so mad as to go and let himself be ruined by those people [the sophists]. That's what they are, the manifest ruin and corruption of anyone who comes into contact with them. (*Meno* 91c)

Socrates: But wouldn't a man like you be ashamed to face your fellow countrymen as a sophist? . . .
Hippocrates: If I am to speak my real mind, I certainly should. (*Protagoras* 312a)

Socrates: I am aware that the Sophists have plenty of brave words and fair conceits, but I am afraid that being only wanderers from one city to another, and having never had habitations of their own, they may fail in their conception of philosophers and statesmen and may not know what they do and say in time of war, when they are fighting or holding parley with their enemies. (*Timaeus* 19e)

Socrates: Each of these private teachers who work for pay, whom the politicians call Sophists and regard as their rivals, inculcates nothing else than these opinions of the multitude which they opine when they are assembled and calls this knowledge wisdom. (*Republic* 6.493a)

Aristotle, perhaps Plato's most famous student, toes the party line, as it were, and his view of sophists and sophistry most resembles the view of Plato's Stranger in *The Sophist*. In *Sophistical Refutations*, Aristotle writes, "The art of the sophist is the semblance of wisdom without the reality, and the sophist is one who makes money from an apparent but unreal wisdom" (165a). And, as George Kennedy's translation of the *Rhetoric* suggests, Aristotle describes sophists in that context as speakers who use "tricky" or "specious" arguments (35–36). And so the scene was set for future rhetoricians to vilify the sophists as opponents to everything right and good—that is, whatever happened to be the popular rhetorical theory of the day—regardless of its actual resemblance to what many of the sophists might have professed. But, happily, not all scholars in antiquity accepted Plato's and Aristotle's versions of the story.

Aristides, a second-century CE Greek rhetorician, traveled extensively, studying rhetoric and philosophy in Asia, Italy, and Egypt, but he spent most of his adult life speaking, writing, and teaching in Athens. Well trained in the rich Athenian oratorical tradition, Aristides was familiar with the teachings of the sophists, and he was well aware of their vexed history in relation to Plato and his followers. Yet even Aristides recognized that the ancient Greek term *sophist* simply meant "wise man," until, that is, Plato and his fourth-century BCE contemporaries changed its usage to a term of reproach. In his *Orations,* Aristides writes:

> Did not Herodotus call Solon a "sophist," and in turn Pythagoras? Did not Androtion call the Seven (I mean the Seven Wise Men) "sophists," and Socrates in turn, that famous individual, a "sophist"? . . . Does not Lysias call Plato a "sophist," and again Aeschines? By way of reproach in the case of Lysias, one might say. But the rest of the authors at any rate were not reproaching those other distinguished individuals; nevertheless, they called them by this name. And further, although it was possible to call Plato a "sophist" by way of reproach, why should anyone speak of those others so? No, I think that "sophist" was probably a general term. . . . (46)

According to Aristides, then, a radical shift in the usage of the term sophist had occurred. Before Plato it was good to be called a sophist, but after Plato it was a source of shame (see Socrates's discussion with Hippocrates in the *Protagoras,* part of which is quoted above). If we are to understand the sophists and consequently the new sophistic rhetoric as fully as we are able, we must understand that Plato's descriptions of the sophists are deceptively specific, limiting the usage of the term to only those traveling teachers with whom he would quarrel, and also inaccurately ascribing to each sophist–character certain qualities and doctrines that the present extant texts may not support.

Yet for centuries after Plato, received wisdom about the sophists was derived largely from the Platonic corpus, and *if* any sophistic text was examined closely, it was most often done through the perspective of a Platonic terministic screen. This received wisdom, however, would begin to change in the twentieth century. According to W. K. C. Guthrie, several historical developments—but especially the horrible events in Germany before and during World War II—created a milieu in which some scholars of ancient philosophy began to rethink the opposition between the sophists and their rival Plato. Guthrie writes:

> Until comparatively recently the prevailing view, the view in which a scholar of my own generation was brought up, was that in his quarrel with the Sophists Plato was right. He was what he claimed to be, the real philosopher or lover of wisdom, and the Sophists were superficial, destructive, and at worst deliberate deceivers, purveyors of sophistry in the modern sense of that term. Since the 1930s, however, we have seen a strong movement to reinstate the Sophists and their kin as champions of progress and enlightenment, and a revulsion from Plato as a bigoted reactionary and authoritarian who by blackening their reputation has insured the suppression of their writings. . . . It is true that the powerful impetus of this movement was given by the rise of totalitarian governments in Europe and the second world war, and it was indeed disturbing to learn that the aim of the German Nazi Party, as described in its official programme, was the production of "guardians in the highest Platonic sense." (10)

One problem with many of these "new" interpretations of sophistic doctrines, however, is that they undertook only a negative deconstruction. In other words, they did not challenge the very doctrines Plato ascribed to the sophists; they accepted these doctrines as historical fact and tried instead to *value* those doctrines differently. They accepted the Plato/sophist opposition but now privileged the sophists over Plato. This is a problem, however, precisely because when we examine the extant texts of the sophists, we find that many of the doctrines Plato ascribed to these traveling teachers were beliefs the actual sophists themselves probably would not have held. And so these "new" interpretations in the first half of the twentieth century revalued sophistic doctrines that Plato, not the sophists themselves, wrote.

Throughout the twenty centuries of the Common Era, there have emerged four critical approaches to the sophists, and I list them here in ascending order of value. First, some scholars take Plato at his word, disparaging the sophists as greedy cheaters. Second, some scholars accept what Plato says about the sophists, but they *value,* rather than disparage, these traveling teachers based on Plato's characterization. Third, some scholars put aside Plato's misrepresentations of the sophists, examining the sophistic texts themselves in order to discover common threads among the most prominent "older" sophists. Fourth, some scholars put aside Plato's misrepresentations of the sophists, examining the sophistic texts themselves in order to understand the unique contributions of each individual sophist in the context of pre-Socratic thought. I believe that any scholarship on the sophists that accepts Plato's dialogues as accurate historical accounts of the beliefs and practices of these traveling teachers is unreliable at best, regardless of whether the historians disparage or value Plato's characterization. However, scholarship that critiques or ignores Plato's misrepresentations in favor of the sophists' own words helps us interpret sophistic doctrines more accurately and fully. Although I am convinced that there is value in exploring the sophists as a loosely related but also disparate group, I believe that the most accurate accounts of sophistic doctrines come from studies of individual sophists.

Neosophistic Rhetoric

During the 1970s and 1980s, scholars in communication studies and English departments across the country were articulating what John Trimbur and others have called a social turn in rhetorical studies, a turn toward social constructionism and (social) epistemic rhetoric. The political commitments that these scholars brought to their disciplines, as well as their concern for recovering marginalized voices in the history of rhetoric, made the sophists an obvious and rich object of analysis. In "Theses on the Philosophy of History," Walter Benjamin writes, "For every image of the past that is not recognized by the present as one of its own concerns threatens to disappear irretrievably" (256). This is, of course, what was happening in the revival of sophistry. In what had come to be known as "the sophists"—those ancient antifoundationalists, champions of democracy, teachers of rhetoric—many scholars found a friend in the fray, ancient validation for the arguments they wanted to make about contemporary rhetoric, arguments that were almost as marginalized, it seemed, as those criticized by Plato over two thousand years hence. However, despite much evidence (both in the sophistic texts themselves and in ancient testimonia like Aristides's) that the ancient sophists were simply wise men with widely varying epistemological beliefs and political commitments, the early movement to recover the sophists from Plato's deceptive representation resulted in certain generalizations that, in the end, have hurt the cause more than they have helped it.

Most symptomatic of the sort of generalizations that were characteristic of the early revival is John Poulakos's influential article "Toward a Sophistic Definition of Rhetoric." Here Poulakos derives a coherent "sophistic" definition of rhetoric that he claims is still relevant: "Rhetoric is the art which seeks to capture in opportune moments that which is appropriate and attempts to suggest that which is possible" (36). And Poulakos claims to draw this definition from the sophists "commonly recognized as the major figures of this group of teachers of rhetoric, that is, Protagoras, Gorgias, Prodicus, Antiphon, Hippias, Critias, and Thrasymachus" (47). The obvious problem with such generalizations, as Edward Schiappa has repeatedly pointed out, is that the historical sophists named by Poulakos were so disparate that these kinds of conclusions about them simply cannot be drawn from any reliable evidence. In fact, Critias, one of the eight sophists listed by Poulakos, was an oligarchic tyrant who led the bloody overthrow of Athenian democracy by the Thirty in 404 BCE. According to N. G. L. Hammond, the views and methods of the Thirty oligarchs were exemplified in two sayings of Critias: "The finest constitution is that of Sparta," the militaristic oligarchy to which Athens had been opposed for decades during the Peloponnesian War, and "All changes of constitution involve bloodshed" (443). During its terrible reign in Athens from 404 to 403 BCE, led by Critias and his assassins, the Thirty executed over 1,500 and banished over 5,000 of their own Greek countrymen (443–44). Critias (and certainly others in Poulakos's list of sophists) would have rejected Poulakos's definition of rhetoric, and so Critias (and others) cannot serve as a model for the contemporary political projects that scholars such as Sharon Crowley, Susan Jarratt, Michael Leff, Roger Moss, Jasper Neel, John Poulakos, and Victor Vitanza choose to pursue.

In 1991, Edward Schiappa entered the debate about sophistic and neosophistic rhetoric with some important correctives. In "Sophistic Rhetoric: Oasis or Mirage," Schiappa argues that what we have come to know as sophistic rhetoric is actually a "mirage—something we see because we want and need to see it—which vaporizes once carefully scrutinized" (5). First, sophistic rhetoric is a mirage because those individuals called sophists before Plato were radically diverse. Thus, "we cannot identify a defining characteristic of 'the sophists' that allows us to narrow the group to a degree sufficient to adduce a common perspective or set of practices" (8). Second, Schiappa argues convincingly that Plato coined the term *rhêtorikê* (the word from which we get rhetoric); the sophists used not rhetoric but *logos* to refer to their art of discourse. But since each sophist had a very different conception of *logos* (compare even the two most famous sophists, Gorgias and Protagoras), we simply cannot suggest that there might be a *common* definition of sophistic rhetoric (8–9). Schiappa concludes that if there *are* good reasons to borrow ideas from the fifth century BCE, then "Let us be explicit about the nature of our debts" (15). Rather than constructing sophistic rhetoric as a generic fiction with little historical validity, let us name the individual sophists with whom we find affinities and in whom we find rich resources. Further, if we appropriate ancient doctrines for contemporary purposes, then labels such as neosophistic signal that "it is we who have formulated the rhetoric" (15).

In "Neo-Sophistic Rhetorical Criticism or the Historical Reconstruction of Sophistic Doctrines?" Schiappa, borrowing terminology from Richard Rorty, differentiates between the historical reconstruction of sophistic doctrines and the rational reconstruction of neosophistic rhetorical theory and criticism, and while "both activities are worthwhile intellectual endeavors, our scholarship can profit by keeping the two distinct" (193). Stephen Makin suggests that a *"historical reconstruction* of some philosopher's thought gives an account of what some past thinker said, or would have said, to his *contemporaries"* but "a *rational reconstruction* treats a thinker (in many cases, dead) as within our own philosophical framework" (qtd. in Schiappa, "Neo-Sophistic" 193–94). Schiappa writes:

> Rational and historical reconstruction differ in terms of *goals* and *methods*. Since the goal of historical reconstruction is to recapture the past insofar as possible on its own terms, the methods of the historian and, in classical work, the philologist, are appropriate. Since the goal of rational reconstruction is to provide critical insight to contemporary theorists, the needs and values of current audiences justify less rigidity and more creativity in the process of interpreting how dead authors through their texts speak to live, contemporary authors. ("Neo-Sophistic" 194)

Finally, Schiappa suggests that scholars who practice neosophistic rhetorical criticism "draw on sophistic thinking in order to contribute to *contemporary* theory and practice. They are examples of 'rational reconstruction' to the extent that their value is measured more on creativity and modern utility than strictly on historical accuracy" (195).

I agree with Schiappa that we must maintain a clear distinction between the goals and methods of historical scholarship that *interprets* ancient doctrines and "neo"historical scholarship that *appropriates* ancient doctrines for contemporary purposes.[1] However, I do have two quarrels with Schiappa's taxonomy. First, I argue that historical and rational reconstruction are fluid points on a continuum, not all-or-nothing categories (see also Vitanza 31), and this continuum is best understood more generally as historical interpretation. Second, the practice of neosophistic appropriation does not fall into the category of rational reconstruction, but instead, since its goals and methods are different from those characteristic of historical interpretation, neosophistic appropriation requires its own category.

In *The Writing of History,* Michel de Certeau argues that the necessarily contingent process of writing history "promotes a selection between what can be *understood* and what must be *forgotten* in order to obtain the representation of a present intelligibility" (4). For de Certeau, the very act of *writing* (anything) is itself an interpretation, a construction, and when we write *histories,* we perform this social act through disciplinary, institutionalized lenses. The past is not comprehensible to the present except through intelligible frameworks; it is simply impossible to reconstruct the past *as it actually was.* As the human mind evolves in response to new technologies and social institutions, its ability to capture the "truth" of the past erodes irretrievably. In other words, we are simply not capable of shedding our literate (Ong) or post-literate electronic (McLuhan) mindsets in order to understand the protoliterate (or still partially oral) discourse theory of the fifth-century BCE Greek sophists, and so we can never fully understand Gorgias's *real* view of *logos* (if such a *real* view ever existed) because we are not fifth-century BCE Greeks. It is in this view of history that the distinctions between historical and rational reconstruction begin to break down.

But this does not mean that what Schiappa and Rorty call historical reconstruction is impossible. Historical reconstructionists consciously attempt to put aside those modern frameworks that they know were not available in the past. In *The Order of Things,* for example, Michel Foucault writes, "Historians want to write histories of biology in the eighteenth century; but they do not realize that biology did not exist then, and that the pattern of knowledge that has been familiar to us for a hundred and fifty years is not valid for a previous period" (127). This is the historical reconstructionist stance toward historiography, and it is also the same stance Schiappa takes toward studies of sophistic rhetoric. In "*Rhêtorikê:* What's in a Name?" Schiappa argues that Plato coined the Greek word *rhêtorikê*. And since rhetoric (that is, the word and thus the discipline) did not exist until the fourth century BCE, it is anachronistic to assume that an art of rhetoric was theorized or even practiced among the fifth-century BCE sophists.

The important thing to remember, however, is that no historians are ever able to take full inventory of (that is, to analyze and bring completely to consciousness) all the modern frameworks that condition their interpretive processes. Karl Popper, a theorist of historical methodology, argues that in any historical interpretation "a point of view is inevitable; and the naïve attempt to avoid it can only lead to self-deception, and to the uncritical application of an unconscious point of view" (261). Thus, I argue that even while Schiappa disparages the search for sophistic *rhetoric,* he is himself, nevertheless, governed by his own twentieth-century thought processes, including the neopragmatist attitude toward history and historiography that he applies to his study of ancient texts. In fact, the very notion of historical reconstruction or objective historiography is a modern invention that the ancient sophists/historians Herodotus and Thucydides did not know.[2]

It is also important to recognize that scholars who engage in what Schiappa and Rorty call rational reconstruction do *not* exclude historical reconstruction from their writing. In other words, the act of rational reconstruction is not simply a process of describing the present using historical data. The past, in whatever imperfect modes of access we have to it, guides rational reconstruction as much as it guides historical reconstruction. Indeed, most of the scholars whom we might classify as historical reconstructionists find *rhetoric* among the sophists, including G. B. Kerferd, W. K. C. Guthrie, N. G. L. Hammond, G. E. R. Lloyd, Tony M. Lentz, and Richard Leo Enos, among many, many others. The fact that these classicists refer to the fifth-century *logôn technê* (the art of *discourse*), as rhetoric *does not,* by default or by association with rational reconstruction, imply any less attention in their scholarship to historical facts than those scholars who do not use the term rhetoric to refer to the sophistic *logôn technê*. Further, while historical reconstructionists attempt to shed modern schemata from their interpretive meth-

ods, a task that is for the most part impossible, some rational reconstructionists acknowledge the inevitability of modern schemata and proceed
with caution. In cultural studies and sociological research, this conscious
acknowledgment of conceptual starting points is called a "theoretical
confession" (Willis 90–91).

Thus, to conclude this discussion of my first quarrel with Schiappa's
taxonomy, I reassert that historical reconstruction and rational reconstruction are fluid points on a continuum, not all-or-nothing categories,
and this continuum is best understood as historical interpretation. Since
any act of rational reconstruction necessarily involves historical reconstruction and since any act of historical reconstruction necessarily involves (unconscious) rational reconstruction, then categorizing historical writing as one-or-the-other becomes difficult, to say the least. Viewed
as two points on the continuum of historical interpretation, historical
reconstruction and rational reconstruction, both of which are present
in all historical writing, become more useful concepts for the social practice of historiography.

My second quarrel with Schiappa's taxonomy has to do with sub-
suming neosophistic appropriation into the category rational reconstruction. I argue that since the practice of neosophistic appropriation has
different goals and methods from those characteristic of historical interpretation, neosophistic appropriation requires its own category. The
fundamental difference between historical interpretation and neosophistic appropriation is this: in historical interpretation writers impose
(consciously or not) modern frameworks on the past, and in neosophistic
appropriation writers search the past for contributions to modern theoretical problems and problematics. In other words, treating a thinker "as
within our own philosophical framework" (Makin; qtd. in Schiappa,
"Neo-Sophistic" 194) does not necessarily imply the practice of appropriation. And while many scholars of sophistic rhetoric practice historical
interpretation for its own sake, there are other scholars of neosophistic
rhetoric who believe that the role of history should be to contribute solutions to present and future problems.

In "Speaking to the Past," for example, Susan Jarratt asks "how
feminists writing histories of rhetoric can take up the challenge . . . to
create histories aimed at a more just future" (190–91). Jarratt's feminist
historiography is not purely historical interpretation (though it is based
largely on it), since her goals and methods do not end with the attempt
to understand ancient doctrines or validate them with reference to modern theory. Instead, Jarratt wants feminists to rewrite history so that new,

more egalitarian historical narratives can feed into and thereby change our present, oppressive narratives. Neosophistic appropriation relies on historical interpretation, but since neosophistic appropriation's historical methodology has a deliberately selective character, it remains fundamentally different from historical interpretation in its goals and methods, and in order for us to fully understand the impact of neosophistic appropriation on contemporary rhetorical studies, it thus requires a category of its own.

Although all neosophists engage in the critical act of appropriation, *not* all neosophists appropriate ancient doctrines in the same way. Just as different critical approaches have emerged in the historical interpretation of sophistic doctrines, so, too, are there different critical approaches among neosophists. First, there are a few neosophists who appropriate Plato's characterization of these traveling teachers, either valuing Plato's misrepresentations or disparaging them (Lanham, for example). Second, there are a few more neosophists who put aside Plato's misrepresentations of sophistic doctrines, appropriating doctrines instead from actual sophistic texts and historical interpretations of them in order to find common threads among the "older sophists" and contemporary composition and rhetorical theorists (Jarratt and John Poulakos, for example). Third, the lion's share of neosophists put aside Plato's misrepresentations of sophistic doctrines, appropriating doctrines instead from actual sophistic texts and historical interpretations of them in order to understand the unique contributions of individual sophists, usually Protagoras and Gorgias, to contemporary rhetorical theory and composition studies (Crowley, Neel, Scott, and Vitanza, to name a few). I will not discuss at length the neosophistic rhetoric of the first variety, since I believe it is not useful or prevalent (that is, because it accepts Plato as an authority on the sophists). And while I do not rigorously retain the distinction between the second and third categories of neosophistic appropriation throughout the rest of this book, it is useful to keep in mind that the more specific the appropriation, the stronger the resulting neosophistic rhetoric. Thus, assuming a clear separation between historical interpretation (with historical reconstruction and rational reconstruction functioning as points on a continuum) and neosophistic appropriation, I proceed, though with caution.

Gorgias and the New Sophistic Rhetoric is my answer (that is, just one of many possible answers) to some of the problems raised in this introduction, as well as many others that will be raised throughout the book as a whole. I have divided the heart of the book into two parts to high-light my separate intentions.

In part one, I engage in the historical interpretation of Gorgianic rhetoric, reading the three primary extant texts (*On Non-Existence,* the *Encomium of Helen,* and the *Defense of Palamedes*) as a holistic state-ment about communal and ethical uses of *logos,* a statement that runs counter to Plato's (mis)representation of it in his dialogue the *Gorgias.* Part one is, in other words, an interpretation of what Gorgias might have said to his contemporaries about the art of rhetoric. The two chapters in this section are concerned exclusively with the doctrines of the soph-ist Gorgias, and I herein self-consciously avoid making insupportable general claims about the sophists as a group. More specifically, in chapter 1, "Disassembling Plato's Critique of Rhetoric in the *Gorgias* (447a–466a)," I argue that Plato misrepresents Gorgias's epistemology as foun-dational (by forcing his dialogic character Gorgias to agree to three stra-tegic binary oppositions), making Gorgias's rhetorical method based on *kairos,* or the right moment, seem absurd. The extant Gorgianic texts, however, tell a different story. Gorgias himself articulated a relativistic epistemology within which his *kairos*-based methodology was perfectly consistent. Next, in chapter 2, "Gorgias and the Art of Rhetoric," I leave behind Plato's dissembling, his argument having been, I hope, at least partially disassembled. In this second chapter, I explicate much more fully the epistemological and methodological aspects of Gorgias's art of rheto-ric through a holistic reading of the extant texts. Here I argue that *On Non-Existence* theorizes the impact external realities have on the human psyche, the *Helen* explores the unethical workings of persuasion on the human psyche, and the *Palamedes* illustrates *topoi* (places) for the in-vention of ethical arguments. Interpreted as a whole, these texts provide the epistemological grounding for a nascent theory of rhetoric, complete with its negative and positive uses.

In part two, I examine and engage in a variety of neosophistic ap-propriations of Gorgianic rhetoric. The three chapters in part two in-terpret what Gorgias might have said to twenty-first-century rhetori-cians, and they explore the contributions certain aspects of Gorgianic rhetoric make to contemporary rhetorical theory and practice. These chapters also do not in any way attempt to define a general neosophistic rhetoric, since that would be a fiction diluted to the point of meaning-lessness. Instead, the chapters in part two pursue a more specific neo-sophistic theory and practice of rhetoric, one based almost exclusively on *Gorgianic* sophistic doctrines. Specifically, in chapter 3, "Neosophistic Rhetorical Theory," I discuss the most influential neosophistic rhetoricians from the revival of sophistry, focusing on their contributions to contemporary rhetorical theory. In chapter 4, "Postmodern Sophistics," I examine Gorgias in light of postmodernism, suggesting that many of the debates currently raging, specifically regarding the politics of representation, are newly staged versions of debates that raged in Athens during the fifth and fourth centuries BCE. Finally, in chapter 5, "The Global Village, Multiculturalism, and the Functions of Sophistic Rhetoric," I focus on what I believe is Gorgias's (and a few other sophists') most important contribution to contemporary rhetoric—*kairos,* or the doctrine of the right moment. Here I examine specifically how the ancient conception of *kairos* might contribute to multiculturalism's political and rhetorical strategies for combating hegemonic discourses.

In *Gorgias and the New Sophistic Rhetoric,* I hope to illuminate aspects of Gorgias's art of rhetoric that have not yet been demonstrated, and I also hope to articulate a *new* sophistic rhetoric based almost exclusively on the sophist Gorgias. This new sophistic rhetoric relies on three basic assumptions: first, knowledge(s) (that is, epistemologies) can only be understood within the defining context of particular cultures; second, rhetorical methods rely, at least in part, on probability, affect, and *kairos*; and third, this relativistic rhetoric of the right moment supports democratic power formations that depend on the invention of ethical arguments. Throughout the following five chapters, different aspects of this new (and old) sophistic rhetoric will come into focus at different times, articulating parts that will lead, I hope, to a coherent whole.

Part One

Historical Interpretation

1
Disassembling Plato's Critique of Rhetoric in the *Gorgias* (447a–466a)

Plato's disdain for sophistic doctrines, especially those concerning rhetoric, is no grand secret. G. B. Kerferd calls Plato's treatment of sophists in general "profoundly hostile" (1). Indeed, throughout the Platonic corpus, sophistic doctrines are criticized, and specifically in the *Gorgias,* the sophist from Leontini, Sicily, is outright ridiculed. Yet, despite Plato's overt distrust of the sophists in general and of Gorgias in particular, some recent scholars find no fault with Plato's treatment of Gorgianic rhetoric in the early pages of the *Gorgias.*

Kathleen Freeman, for example, maintains that "the opinions on rhetoric attributed to [Gorgias] by Plato are probably genuine" (*Pre-Socratic* 366). Similarly, in the introductions to their respective editions of Plato's *Gorgias,* both Terence Irwin and W. H. Thompson claim that the sophist Gorgias is accurately represented, that the ideas of the historical figure match those of Plato's character. According to Irwin, Plato was attempting to portray Gorgias as a historical character complete with all of his real inconsistencies, and "judged this way, the portrayal seems plausible" (9–10). Thompson claims that Plato's treatment of Gorgias "in this dialogue is respectful rather than contumelious," and "if this dialogue had been lost, and the works of Gorgias had come down to us entire, there is reason to doubt whether his reputation would have stood so high as it does at present" (iv–v). Renato Barilli argues that in the *Gorgias,* the Leontinian sophist is treated with dignity and fairness (8) and that "Plato had skillfully expounded the point of view of the Sophists in [the] *Gorgias* . . ." (30). Michael C. Leff suggests that the

Gorgias "perceptively locates essential features of sophistic rhetoric and recognizes clearly the threat they pose to [Plato's] own philosophical program. Ironically, then, it is one of the best available sources for reconstructing the thought of the ancient sophists" ("Modern" 36). Donald Clark also argues that "Plato is not too unfair in attributing to Gorgias this narrow limitation of the field of rhetoric" (28). John Burnet claims that "it is not Plato's way to introduce fictitious characters" (121). Finally, perhaps the most naïve comment of all is attributable to G. C. Field: "Because it is a real conversation, the views discussed [in the *Gorgias*] represent actual views of individual people" (xii). Unfortunately, the acceptance of Plato's treatment of Gorgianic doctrines—especially those regarding the art of *logos*—has resulted in an impoverished contemporary view of Gorgias and his rhetorical *technê*.[1]

In this chapter, I engage in what I have called historical interpretation, arguing for a conception of Gorgianic rhetoric that is very different from Plato's version. When the extant texts of Gorgias are examined closely, abandoning the "aid" of Plato's dialogues, we discover theoretical coherence and practical validity where there was once thought to be only contradiction and deceit. The extant texts reveal that Gorgias's epistemology is relativistic, and his corresponding rhetorical methodology works to seize the opportune moment *(kairos)* in which certain kinds of language can be used to unite subjective consciousnesses into a communal desire for action. Gorgias's rhetorical methodology, based in part on *kairos,* requires a relativistic epistemology that allows for the determination of communal truth through the consensus of many. *Kairos* cannot function as the basis of a rhetorical methodology within a foundational epistemology, since any time is the "right time" when one possesses truth. In the *Gorgias,* however, Plato misrepresents the Leontinian sophist as having a foundational epistemology while retaining Gorgias's *kairos*-governed methodology, making him appear contradictory and absurd.

The purpose of this first chapter is to reveal Plato's motivations and methods for misrepresenting Gorgias. First, I will examine Plato's writer–audience relationship with the Athenian citizenry around the date that he published the *Gorgias,* revealing some of the economic, political, and social exigencies that led Plato to misrepresent the sophist Gorgias's epistemology. Finally, I will analyze the methods Plato employs to misrepresent the epistemology of Gorgias, and I will defend Gorgias against Plato's critique of rhetoric through reference to the extant Gorgianic texts.

The Historical Situation

When Plato wrote the *Gorgias,* the Athenian democracy was in an unstable condition. E. R. Dodds convincingly places the date of the *Gorgias's* composition at around 387 BCE (*Plato* 24)—just twenty-four years after the tyranny of the Four Hundred and just seventeen years after the tyranny of the Thirty. Alcibiades and Critias, two of Socrates's most successful students, led the revolutions in the waning years of the Peloponnesian War that resulted in these bloody oligarchic tyrannies, and their antidemocratic exploits contributed much to the Athenian death sentence against their mentor Socrates.[2]

According to Thucydides, in 411 BCE Alcibiades persuaded many of the war-weary Athenian troops that he could arrange a peace treaty between Athens and their Spartan enemies (a questionable claim since Alcibiades was instrumental in breaking Athens's truce with Sparta just seven years earlier). Alcibiades's peace treaty, however, would contain one necessary condition: that Athens restructure its democratic government into an oligarchic system of four hundred rulers (8.45–49). Soon after this oligarchy took power, Alcibiades, not surprisingly, failed in his attempts to secure peace with Sparta (8.70–71). As dissension from vocal democrats increased, the oligarchs began putting to death anyone who dared speak against the present government (8.72–73). Finally realizing the deceit Alcibiades used to gain power, the failure of his attempts at securing peace, and the brutality he employed to retain his power, the reinvigorated democratic sentiments of the Athenian citizens incited them to overthrow Alcibiades and his oligarchic colleagues. The bloody oligarchy was over, and Athens returned to democracy (8.74–81).

The tyranny of the Thirty in 404 BCE, led by Socrates's student Critias, was even bloodier than the tyranny of the Four Hundred. As Xenophon tells us, having received several regiments of fresh troops from supportive Spartan allies, Critias and the other oligarchic tyrants set up a government of thirty rulers (plus twenty-one powerful economic advisors) and three thousand citizens—all other residents of Athens were allowed no legal rights whatsoever. Two fates often befell those middle- and lower-class residents of Athens who were not listed among the 3,051 citizens protected by the laws of the oligarchic government: many of them had their properties confiscated, and others were murdered for publicly opposing the Thirty (*Hellenica* 2.3.11–21).

Having removed legal rights from middle- and lower-class residents of Athens, Critias and the rest of the Thirty began to make more specific the ambiguous laws that Solon had written for the Athenian democracy (Krentz 62); ambiguous laws require deliberation that empowers those who possess rhetorical skills over those with mere wealth and high birth. In fact, Critias was so leery of rhetorical prowess among the masses that he wrote a law forbidding instruction in *logôn technê*, the art of discourse (Xenophon, *Memorabilia* 1.2.31).[3]

A few months after the forced installation of the oligarchic Thirty, Thrasybulus and about seventy other exiled Athenian democrats marched toward Athens and defeated the oligarchs despite their Spartan troops, killing many of the Thirty, Critias among them, in battle. Athens again returned to democratic rule (*Hellenica* 2.4.2–43).

In democratic Athens, following 404 BCE, oligarchic sentiment was treated with caution, as when Socrates was tried by Miletus for corrupting the youth of Athens. Indeed, during the trial itself Miletus mentioned the brutal oligarchs Alcibiades and Critias as the most prominent of these corrupted youth (Xenophon, *Memorabilia* 1.2.9–12). And soon after Socrates drank the hemlock, Plato, certainly Socrates's most famous student, began to challenge democracy—favoring, of course, oligarchy—and attacking rhetoric and its teachers.

Plato's desire for oligarchic government in Athens rested on his foundational epistemology. Access to true knowledge was limited to those of wealth and high birth, and those few born with these qualities were the only legitimate candidates to be counted among the philosophic ruling few. Many of the sophists, on the other hand, favored the Athenian democracy the way it was, and their desire for democracy rested on their relativistic epistemologies. The relativistic sophists believed that knowledge is unstable and that laws and policies *(nomoi)* grow out of discussion. For many of these sophists, and especially Gorgias, opinions are communal and governed by language *(logos)*. Thus, rhetoric supplies the necessary tools for mastery over opinion and, consequently, the ability for anyone to function effectively in a democratic society. All people, claimed certain sophists, are able to learn how collaboratively to govern a city *(polis)* and nobility of birth and high economic status are irrelevant.

Plato must have been concerned about the Athenian audience who would read the *Gorgias* in 387 BCE. Most Athenian citizens, when Plato wrote the dialogue, were anti-oligarchy, with the bitter memory of Socrates's students Alcibiades and Critias fresh in their minds. At that time, few Athenian readers of the *Gorgias* would have judged in Socrates's favor had Plato presented Gorgias's beliefs as he truly would have expressed them. Thus, in order to win the inevitably hostile Athenian democrats over to the side of philosophy (from rhetoric), Plato presented Gorgias's *technê* as though it had arisen out of an epistemology grounded on the belief in extralinguistic, *a priori* truths and certain knowledge—both of which are assumptions that Gorgias would have flatly rejected. As I intend to demonstrate, Plato's purpose in the *Gorgias* was to present the Leontinian sophist as a rhetorician with a foundational epistemology so that his *kairos*-governed *technê,* effective under democratic rule, would seem absurd.

Disassembling Plato's Critique

In his speech to Polus, following his dialectical interaction with Gorgias, Socrates claims a meager place for rhetoric in the activities of human life—that it is to the soul what cookery is to the body—through three basic assertions: (1) rhetoric is not an art *(technê)* because it is irrational *(alogon)* (*Gorgias* 464e–465a); (2) rhetoric is flattery *(kolakeia)* because its goal is to elicit pleasure *(terpsis)* without concern for the greatest good *(beltistos)* (465a); and (3) rhetoric is a knack *(tribê)* because it cannot articulate its methods or their causes *(aitiai)* (465a). In order to validate this three-part claim, Socrates must coax Gorgias into accepting three respective binary oppositions: (1) knowledge *(epistêmê* or *mathêsis)* versus opinion *(doxa* or *pistis)*, (2) instruction *(didachê)* versus persuasion *(peithô)*, and (3) language *(logos)* versus content *(pragma)* in the definition of a *technê*.[4] Although Plato's Gorgias readily assents to any claim Socrates cares to make, a closer look at the extant Gorgianic texts reveals the absurdity in the assertion that Gorgias the sophist would have uttered agreement with any of Socrates's claims about rhetoric or any of the binary oppositions that Socrates sets up to make those claims.[5]

Socrates's first major claim about rhetoric, that it is not a *technê* because it is irrational, is legitimate within the world of the dialogue because Plato's Gorgias agrees to the binary opposition of knowledge versus opinion. The only way for Plato to succeed in claiming that rhetoric is irrational is to make Gorgias concede that there exists such a concept as the "rational." For Plato, the rational is based on certain knowledge of immutable truth; it is to an eternal image or form, discoverable only through negative dialectic, that arguments may be compared in order to determine their rational or irrational character. Mere belief, according to Plato, cannot be based on immutable truth (otherwise it would be knowledge); thus, when compared to any relevant eternal image or form, opinion proves irrational, inconsistent with absolute truth and pure knowledge. Plato writes:

> *Socrates:* Is there a state which you call "having learned"?
> *Gorgias:* There is.
> *Socrates:* And such a thing as "having believed"?
> *Gorgias:* There is.
> *Socrates:* Now, do you think that to have learned and to have believed, or knowledge *[mathêsis]* and belief *[pistis]*, are one and the same or different?
> *Gorgias:* I consider them different, Socrates. (*Gorgias* 454c–454d)

Plato's Gorgias agrees that knowledge (the rational) and opinion (the irrational) exist simultaneously, and his assent to this point haunts him when Socrates asks what sort of effect rhetoric has on its audience: Gorgias concedes that his *technê* merely creates belief and does not provide knowledge of what is right and wrong (454d–454e). Thus, Plato's Gorgias allows Socrates to claim that Gorgianic rhetoric is irrational, that it does not refer to an immutable standard of truth, and so it does not qualify as a *technê*.

But for Gorgias the sophist, there can be no rational or irrational arguments because all human beliefs and communicative situations are relative to a particular *kairos* or "right moment," and according to Gorgias, the *kairos* of any given situation is not attainable through pure knowledge. In his *Encomium of Helen*, Gorgias writes:

> If all people on all subjects had memory of things past and comprehension of things present and prescience of things to come, then language *[logos]* would not function as it does [that is, as an imprecise medium]; however, the way things are, it is difficult to remember the past and perceive the present and foretell the future, so that most people regarding most subjects accept opinion *[doxa]* as advisor to their soul *[psuchê]*. (B11.11)[6]

For Gorgias, perfect knowledge of the past, present, and future is impossible. Thus, since rationality depends on some sort of reference to perfect knowledge in order to judge its legitimacy, no argument can ever be entirely rational in the Platonic sense of the word. In *Kaironomia: On the Will-to-Invent*, Eric Charles White also connects Gorgias's rejection of Platonic rationalism to the sophistic belief in *kairos*:

For Gorgias, *kairos* stands for a radical principle of occasionality which implies a conception of the production of meaning in language as a process of continuous adjustment to and creation of the present occasion, or a process of continuous *interpretation* in which the speaker seeks to inflect the given "text" to his or her own ends at the same time that the speaker's text is "interpreted" in turn by the context surrounding it. This subordination of meaning to occasion entails the view that the truth of an utterance is immanent and not anterior to the situation of the utterance itself. In other words, the persuasive force of a speech does not derive from its correspondence to a preexisting reality or truth. Truth is relative to the speaker and the immediate context. There is no criterion or standard that might once and for all found and orient the progress of knowledge. The persuasive force of the truth must be renewed at each occasion and cannot become, therefore, a routine accomplishment. (14–15)

In a rhetorical *technê* that is governed by *kairos,* then, one must, of necessity, articulate and adhere to a relativistic epistemology, for why would one adjust one's rhetoric to a context when the truth of the matter already exists external to the rhetorical situation?

Gorgias's relativistic epistemology legitimates his claim that pure knowledge does not exist and that no *logos* can be wholly rational. Sextus Empiricus summarizes Gorgias's famous statement on epistemological instability:

In what is titled *On Non-Existence* or *On Nature,* Gorgias develops three sequential arguments: first and foremost, that nothing exists; second, that even if existence exists, it is inapprehensible to humans; and, third, that even if existence is apprehensible, nevertheless it is certainly not able to be communicated or interpreted for one's neighbors. (B3.65)

This epistemology is the grounding for Gorgias's belief in the distorting process of sensory perception, making Socrates's knowledge-versus-opinion binary unacceptable for Gorgias the sophist. Gorgias refers often in *On Non-Existence* to "things that actually exist" *(ta onta),* or perceptibles, which reveals his belief in a reality external to human interpretation. It is, however, the process of human perceptual interaction with these realities that negates the possibility for certain knowledge (and rationality) in the Platonic sense. Gorgias writes, "If things-being-thought do not exist, then existence is not thought" (B3.77); therefore, "Existence is not thought or perceived" (B3.82). Humans can only think *about* things; they cannot think the things themselves. Thus, once a real thing is perceived by a human, it ceases to exist in a real sense, thereby distorting the existential nature of the thing perceived. Gorgias's view that the act of human perception distorts reality allows him to deny the possibility of pure knowledge and atemporal rational thought. Platonic rational thought relies on the ability to refer to some external reality or immutable truth in order for it to progress rationally. However, since, for Gorgias, external perceptibles are constantly susceptible to distortion in the human sensory-perception process, no human thought can ever be considered "rational."

To further complicate the matter, however, it is clear that Gorgias *did* believe in certain conceptions of "knowledge" and "truth," and in some circumstances "opinion" was insufficient. In fact, Gorgias uses the term *alêtheia* (the same word Plato uses to mean "truth") in both the *Palamedes* and the *Helen,* and specifically in the *Palamedes,* Gorgias sets "truth" *(alêtheia)* and "knowledge" (Gorgias uses various grammatical forms of the word *eidô*) in opposition to "opinion" *(doxa).* In the *Palamedes,* Gorgias's title character argues that Odysseus has falsely accused him of treason, and he continues:

> Thus you clearly do not possess knowledge *(oistha,* a form of *eidô)* of the crimes of which you accuse me. It follows that since you do not possess knowledge *(eidota),* you possess an opinion *(doxadzein).* So, then, most reckless of all men, trusting in opinion *(doxêi),* a most untrustworthy thing, not knowing *(eidôs)* the truth *(alêtheian),* do you recklessly seek the death penalty for a man? . . . But certainly all men may possess opinions *(doxasai)* on all matters, and in this respect you have no more wisdom than others. But it is wrong to trust those with an opinion *(doxadzousi)* instead of those who know *(eidosin)* and to consider opinion *(doxan)* more believable than truth *(alêtheias),* but truth *(alêtheian)* rather than opinion *(doxês).* (B11a.24)

This is certainly a difficult passage with which to contend if we rely only on the English translation since both Plato and Gorgias appear to use and favor the word *knowledge.* However, it is clear from the Greek terms that Gorgias's word for knowledge *(eidô)* is different from Plato's word *(epistêmê)* for the same English concept of knowledge. Plato's term *epistêmê*, on the one hand, implies an understanding that exists prior to any given situation in which it might be applied. Gorgias's term *eidô*, on the other hand, implies an understanding that is derived empirically from a situation, and its etymology is related to sight. Thus, Plato refers to *a priori* knowledge *(epistêmê)*, which is consistent with the requirements of his foundational epistemology, and Gorgias refers to empirical knowledge *(eidô)*, which is consistent with the requirements of his relativistic epistemology. For Gorgias, knowledge that is gained empirically through communal discourse in public rhetorical situations is more reliable than purely subjective opinions, and, as I will argue more thoroughly in the next chapter, Gorgias's notion of truth is also particular to cultural contexts, and it is therefore also consistent with his relativistic epistemology.

Socrates's foundational epistemology allows for the knowledge of immutable truth and Gorgias's relativistic epistemology does not. Had Plato presented Gorgias's epistemology accurately, most fourth-century BCE Athenian citizens would have preferred Gorgias's arguments, since democracy depends on the ability to change the opinions of others and the willingness to allow one's own opinions to be changed. For Athenian citizens to admit to the possibility of perfect knowledge—attainable only through Platonic negative dialectic—would require them also to deny the validity of their own democratic power structure. Thus, in order to gain the approval of his anti-oligarchy Athenian audience, Plato misrepresented Gorgias's epistemology. Plato's Gorgias admits to the possibility of knowledge and rational thought, to which only someone with a foundational epistemology could admit. He then concedes that his own notion of rhetoric creates mere opinion (as opposed to knowledge) in his audiences. Plato, therefore, creates a Gorgias with a foundational epistemology and a *kairos*-governed methodology, making Gorgias appear not only irrational but also absurd.

Socrates's second major claim about rhetoric, that it is mere flattery because its goal is to elicit pleasure without concern for the greatest good, is legitimate within the world of the dialogue because Plato's Gorgias agrees to the binary opposition of instruction versus persuasion. Since Plato's Gorgias has agreed that there is knowledge (the rational) and opinion (the irrational), then it follows that there must also be instruction, which results in knowledge, and persuasion, which results in irrational belief. In Plato's *Gorgias,* the Leontinian sophist says that the rhetorician will be more persuasive than the expert "before a crowd."

Socrates replies, then, "among the ignorant, for surely, among those who know he will not be more convincing than the [expert]." Plato's Gorgias agrees that the rhetor lacks the true knowledge possessed by the expert, and so Plato's Gorgias must also agree to Socrates's claim that "the ignorant [rhetorician] is more convincing among the ignorant [crowds] than the expert" (459a–459b). With Gorgias's unfortunate assent, Socrates's claim that Gorgias merely persuades and does not instruct takes special significance. Plato writes:

> *Socrates:* Then rhetoric apparently is a creator of conviction
>   that is persuasive but not instructive about right and wrong.
> *Gorgias:* Yes.
> *Socrates:* Then the rhetorician too does not instruct courts and
>   other assemblies about right and wrong, but is able only to
>   persuade them. (*Gorgias* 455a)

Socrates believes that knowledge of immutable truth (the greatest good) is the goal of negative-dialectical instruction, since one who knows the truth about justice will never act unjustly (460b–460c). Thus, as Plato would have us believe, Socrates's *technê* for moving audiences to action is philosophical (not rhetorical) and the direct result of pure knowledge (not communal opinion).

Obviously Gorgias's rhetorical methodology cannot be called instruction if we accept Plato's definition of the term, since the prerequisite for instruction is pure knowledge, and, as we have already seen, Gorgias the sophist rejects the notion of absolute knowledge, articulating instead a belief in relativistic, communal truth governed by the historical moment. For Gorgias the sophist, any use of language *(logos)* at all is inherently problematic, eliminating any possibility for instruction in universal truth. Gorgias writes in *On Non-Existence*:

> *Logos* is the means by which we communicate, but *logos* is
> different from substances and existent things. Thus we do not
> communicate existent things to our neighbors; instead we
> communicate only *logos*, which is something other than sub-
> stances. (B3.84)

In other words, even if truth—external to context—existed and humans could perceive it, the use of *language* to convey the content of truth, even via dialectical instruction, would result in a degree of communicative uncertainty. In the *Palamedes,* Gorgias reinforces this view of language when Palamedes says:

If, then, by means of argument [dia tôn logôn], the truth [alêtheian] of actions could become free of doubt <and> clear to hearers, judgment would be easy from what has already been said. But since this is not the case, guard my body, deliberate longer, and decide with truth [alêtheias]. (B11a.35)

Here Gorgias (through the mouthpiece of Palamedes) recognizes the unstable character of language and begs his jury to deliberate long, to discuss the matter as a community, and to arrive at a decision through thoughtful discourse. Platonic "instruction" is impossible, and if it were, there would be little need for law courts and politicians.

Yet I also argue that Gorgias's methodology cannot be called persuasion *if* persuasive discourse operates in the realm of individual opinions and not necessarily communal truths. Gorgias writes often of the negative influences of persuasion; indeed, as I will argue more thoroughly in the next chapter, the *Helen* is all about the negative effects of persuasion (divine persuasion, violent persuasion, and lustful persuasion), and *logos* is just one persuasive force with potentially negative uses. Gorgias writes, "Many people have persuaded and continue to persuade many others of many things through inventing false arguments" (B11.11). But just because language is unstable, Gorgias argues, rhetors are not free to use its persuasive power to deceive an audience beyond all reasoning *(logismon)*. Also in the *Helen*, Gorgias declares that it is "the duty of the same man [that is, Gorgias] both to declare what he should rightly and to refute <what has been spoken falsely>" (B11.2). In the *Palamedes,* Gorgias's title character says, "It is wrong to persuade such ones as you with the aid of friends or sorrowful prayers or appeals to pity, but it is right for me, professing truth and not deceiving, to escape this charge by means of the clearest justice" (B11a.33). We must keep in mind, however, that what is "right" and "true" and what is "false" and "deceptive" are all determined by the discourse (both poetic and rhetorical) on Helen and her abduction to Troy and on Palamedes and Odysseus's charge of treason. For Gorgias, reasoning and truth, as White has already demonstrated, are relative to the historical (whether real or poetic) exigencies of a particular rhetorical situation, and Gorgias's claims to reasoning and truth are purely contextual. If the aim of persuasion, then, is to change people's minds for the good of a few, then Gorgias does not practice persuasion—he practices, instead, rhetoric.

I argue that Gorgianic rhetoric *is* concerned with the greatest good, contrary to what Plato would have us believe—but it is the good of the community. And he is also concerned with accomplishing this communal greatest good through affective (though not exclusively pleasurable) discourse. Gorgias's *technê* for moving audiences to action is aesthetic, using the emotional response of an audience to the immediate rhetorical context. To demonstrate reason and truth in the relative context of a particular situation is important; yet it is also important for rhetorical uses of language to elicit a certain emotional response in the audience. According to Charles P. Segal, Gorgianic rhetoric is a two-step process in which *terpsis,* a passive, aesthetic, sensory response to a stimulus, leads to and must precede *anankê,* the active, psyche-based force that motivates the desired physical action in the audience (106–17). First, in *terpsis,* reality is perceived by the interpreting senses (*logos* or *opsis,* for example). *Logos* involves the auditory senses used in interpreting linguistic signals, and *opsis* involves the visual senses used in interpreting colors and shapes. The perception of reality in the human sensory realm leads to aesthetic dissonance *(tarachê)* in the senses. This aesthetic dissonance must precede the active second step in the process of Gorgianic rhetoric, *anankê*. Sensory *tarachê* transfers directly to the *psuchê* and causes it to experience dissonance as well, and this psychic dissonance elicits an immediate submission to an affective response that directly motivates the audience to the desired physical action (106–17). Thus, Plato's claim—that the goal of Gorgias's rhetoric is to elicit pleasure in the audience—is partly true. Gorgias's *technê* is aesthetic, and eliciting pleasure is one aspect of it, but the primary goal of Gorgias's *technê* is the desired action of the audience, and this desired action can only be achieved through eliciting and surpassing an initial, aesthetic response in his audience.

For Gorgias, the nature of human sense perception and its effects on communication necessitate an aesthetic *technê*. For Plato's Socrates, the nature of immutable truth and its effects on negative-dialectical instruction necessitate a knowledge-based *technê*. But the majority of the fourth-century BCE Athenian audience for Plato's *Gorgias* were proponents of democracy who believed strongly in the powers of *logos*. Plato's *technê* of the greatest good is foundational, and only the philosophic ruling few in Plato's oligarchic social and political structure would be able to achieve it. Had Plato presented Gorgias's aesthetic *technê* based on the effects that the distorting process of sensory perception has on human communication, then Plato's fourth-century BCE Athenian audience may have judged the argument between Gorgias and Socrates in favor of Gorgias. Knowing it would be best to avoid such a negative response, Plato again misrepresented Gorgias as having a foundational epistemology. Since Plato's Gorgias accepts that instruction and persuasion exist simultaneously, he must also admit to the existence of immutable truth. Consequently, from the essentialist perspective that Plato's Gorgias adopts, the notion of a rhetorical methodology that focuses on aesthetic response is indeed absurd.

Socrates's third major claim about rhetoric, that it is merely a knack because it cannot articulate its methods or their causes, is legitimate within the world of the dialogue since Gorgias agrees to the binary opposition of language versus content in the definition of an art. For Plato, all arts comprise both extralinguistic content and language, the latter of which, through *a priori* rules and techniques, conveys this content. Plato's Gorgias agrees that rhetoric's effect is secured through language *(logos)*, but he also claims that its content *(pragma)* is twofold: (1) words, or *logoi* (449d) and (2) the greatest and noblest of human affairs (451d). Gorgias explains to Socrates that the contents of the arts other than rhetoric (medicine, physical training, painting, sculpture, etc.) are "concerned with manual crafts," but rhetoric "deals with no such manual product but all its activity and all it accomplishes is through the medium of words *[logoi]*" (450b–450c). Thus, rhetoric's content is not merely describable physical activity; rather, it concerns the timely use of language, which is a necessary component in the content of the art of rhetoric.

In typical Platonic fashion, however, soon after Plato's Gorgias explains his position, the Leontinian sophist accepts Socrates's claim that a *technê* must include extralinguistic content and the language to convey it (453a–455a). Having already coaxed Gorgias into admitting that his own rhetorical methodology includes *logos* in its content (449d), Socrates may then legitimately deny *technê* status to Gorgianic rhetoric. In Plato's notion of art, language is used to articulate the methods of the *technê*'s content and the causes that enable the *technê* to function— since content cannot articulate itself. In Plato's *Phaedrus,* Socrates and his student conclude that successful rhetoric (that is, philosophical rhetoric) presupposes absolute knowledge of the subject at hand (260a). Socrates warns Phaedrus that if he neglects philosophy, then he will never be a competent speaker on any subject because he will lack the means to discover the truth about it (261a). Intensive study of truth legitimates rhetoric for Plato, but the study of language itself, as in sophistic rhetoric, dooms the art of *logos* to operate merely on *doxa,* opinion. And in the *Gorgias,* because Plato's Leontinian sophist places language in the content of his rhetorical *technê* and since this content cannot articulate

itself, rhetoric's methods and causes must remain unknown and incom-
municable. This argument, however, is only valid when the binary opposition of language versus content in the definition of an art is accepted.
And, as usual, Plato's Gorgias readily accepts the binary opposition.

Yet Gorgias the sophist would not have accepted this language-ver-
sus-content opposition in the definition of an art; he believed that *logos*
could be part of both the content and the articulatory method of a *technê*.
According to Segal, the content of Gorgias the sophist's *technê* is twofold: (1) the formal aspect of the *logos* and (2) its effects on the human
senses and *psuchê* (106–28). For Gorgias, language *(logos)* exists as a
system that is available for use when the situation or need arises, at which
time certain formal techniques can be applied to language in order to
secure a desired effect in an audience. In the *Helen,* for example, Gorgias
suggests that in order to prove Helen's critics false and show the truth
of the matter, he would have to give a certain reasoning *(logismon)* to
his language *(logos).* Language alone, in other words, does not fit the
demands of this particular rhetorical situation—there must be reasoning added to the language as well. Poetry, according to Gorgias, is *logos*
with meter (B11.9), not just *logos;* and when *logos* is chanted as divine
incantations, the words become extremely powerful (B11.10). Gorgias
also suggests that when persuasion *(peithô)* gives shape to language
(logos), it "forms the mind as it wishes," and in order to understand the
power of persuasion in combination with *logos,* one must study the discourses of astronomers, public debaters, and philosophers (B11.13). This
double perspective (that is, first, of language as a system, or *logos,* and
second, of certain additions to *logos,* such as reason, meter, chant, and
persuasion) allows Gorgias to both study rhetorical techniques as they
are applied to language and also choose the proper techniques for each
given rhetorical situation.

Further, because Gorgias's epistemology is relativistic and governed
by *kairos,* his *technê* is empirical; since no two aesthetic, formal aspects
of any *logos* will be effective in any two kairotic situations, Gorgias's
technê involves empirically testing and implementing in each individual
communicative situation the linguistic rhetorical choices that are, at that
particular time and place, most effective. Thus, it is necessary for the
Gorgianic orator to know and be able to apply all of the different rhetorical techniques to any *logos* in any kairotic situation. In Gorgianic
rhetoric, it is the formal aspect of the *logos* that causes the state of *tarachê*
in the auditory senses and thus transfers this state of *tarachê* to the
psuchê. Consequently, the second aspect of Gorgias's rhetorical *technê*

is to analyze and know the different types of *psuchai* that exist and to empirically test in each kairotic communicative situation what *metra* of the *logos* are most effective. Therefore, the methods and their causes of Gorgias's empirical *technê* can be articulated only within a kairotic context, but these methods cannot apply to ahistorical situations, as Plato would have them.

In chapter 2, I discuss in detail the role that the *Palamedes* plays in Gorgias's articulation of his rhetorical methods and their causes; however, since this point is also relevant to my current argument, let me briefly forecast that discussion. In the *Palamedes,* Gorgias illustrates the effect of a particular rhetorical situation (Odysseus's claim that Palamedes committed treason) on the ethical invention of arguments from probability; further, these arguments are divided into sections that illustrate *topoi* for inventing arguments that (1) explore past, present, and future probabilities, (2) describe the character of the speakers, and (3) limit the ethical uses of emotion in forensic discourse. Thus, we see from the ancient fragments themselves that, despite the uncertain nature of a rhetoric based on *kairos,* Gorgias was, nevertheless, able to articulate specific rhetorical methods, as long as those methods were articulated in reference to the particular exigencies of a rhetorical situation.

Plato is able to claim that rhetoric is to the soul what cookery is to the body through three assertions: that Gorgianic rhetoric is irrational, only concerned with pleasure, and unable to articulate its methods and their causes. Plato can make these arguments based on his character Gorgias's acceptance of three respective binary oppositions: knowledge versus opinion, instruction versus persuasion, and language versus content in the definition of an art. However, by examining the extant texts of Gorgias, using historical interpretation as a methodological guide, it becomes clear that Gorgias the sophist would not have accepted any of Socrates's three claims about rhetoric because his relativistic epistemology could not support their three corresponding binary oppositions.

Denying *technê* status to Gorgias's notion of *logos* denigrates rhetoric, the primary vehicle of the Athenian democracy, and it valorizes its counterpart negative dialectic, the primary vehicle of the oligarchic power structures in 411 and 404 BCE. Thus, since Plato's audience for the *Gorgias* was largely democratic in political orientation, he misrepresented Gorgias's epistemology in order to ease the anticipated hostility toward the text and to make Gorgianic rhetoric appear absurd.

2
Gorgias and the Art of Rhetoric

In this chapter, I continue the historical interpretation of Gorgias's art of rhetoric, leaving behind Plato's misrepresentations and engaging instead in a detailed and holistic reading of the three primary extant Gorgianic texts. I argue here that these three texts—*On Non-Existence* (or *On Nature*), the *Encomium of Helen,* and the *Defense of Palamedes*—are not disparate or contradictory statements, as is often assumed, but can be read as intricately interrelated and internally consistent contributions to an emerging complex theory and art *(technê)* of rhetoric. Of course, we cannot argue that Gorgias composed these texts with a holistic rhetorical task in mind; however, reconstructing and interpreting *On Non-Existence,* the *Helen,* and the *Palamedes* holistically does shed significant new light on our current understanding of Gorgias's emerging theory and *technê*. In brief, *On Non-Existence* describes the effects that externally given atechnical realities *(ta onta)* have on the human psyche *(psuchê),* the *Helen* explores the unethical workings of the persuasive arts on the human *psuchê,* and the *Palamedes* demonstrates rhetorical *topoi* for the invention of arguments designed to move the human *psuchê* of a forensic audience to ethical action. Reconstructed thus as a holistic statement, Gorgias's primary extant texts theorize the social nature of linguistic symbols and explore their artistic uses for both unethical and ethical purposes; and as a holistic interpretation of the extant texts demonstrates, Gorgias favors the topical invention of ethical arguments over the magical invention of false arguments, unsupported opinions, and deliberate deceptions.

Criticism of Gorgianic rhetoric as inartistic is almost as ancient as the very texts themselves. Plato, who probably wrote some of his earliest dialogues while Gorgias was still living and teaching in Athens, argues in the *Gorgias* that rhetoric is not a *technê* but merely a false art, no more than a form of flattery. Moreover, in the *Phaedrus* Plato explains that sophistic rhetoric is irrational and thus atechnical because it is not founded on truth discovered through the principles of philosophical dialectic. No activity, according to Plato, is artistic unless it begins with a foundation of universal knowledge discovered through dialectical inquiry, and it is precisely because those who claim to teach and practice the art of rhetoric "are ignorant of dialectic that they are incapable of properly defining rhetoric, and that in turn leads them to imagine that by possessing themselves of the requisite antecedent learning they have discovered the art itself" (269b). But if we accept Plato's philosophy/rhetoric demarcation, along with the claim that all arts *(technai)* have their foundation in absolute truth, then there is no possibility for an *art of rhetoric* (or of anything else) except by way of dialectic, a convenient fiction and lucrative advertising for Plato's academy.

While Plato opposes rhetoric, the false art, to dialectic, the true art, Aristotle describes rhetoric as the *antistrophos* (commonly translated "counterpart" but more accurately rendered "correlative" or "coordinate") to dialectic. Kennedy argues that in the very first sentence of the *Rhetoric,* Aristotle refutes Plato's opposition of rhetoric and dialectic (that is, philosophy) in the *Gorgias* (28–29), turning Aristotle at least partly in the theoretical direction of sophistic rhetoric. Although in most instances, according to Aristotle, truth is preferable to probability, a claim that Gorgias also makes in the *Helen* and the *Palamedes,* there are nevertheless realms of human experience in which truth does not always participate. In the *Rhetoric,* Aristotle argues that all human actions, the subjects of rhetorical deliberation and judgment, are based on probability rather than truth (1.2.14). Politics, for example, requires collaborative inquiry into the social needs of a *polis* as a relative response to both the internal and external requirements of particular economic, political, and cultural situations; and the judicial process requires collaborative inquiry into the relative just or unjust nature of human actions according to socially written laws with their attending relative provisions for punishment. Politics and law have their foundations in socially relative customs *(nomoi)* based on communal truths-as-probabilities rather than universal truth; thus the conduct of political and judicial institutions requires an art that derives its power from probability (that is, rhetoric) and not from universal truth (that is, philosophy). And the practice of rhetoric as an art of probability supports democratic political and legal institutions since

important decisions require articulations of multiple perspectives and critical debates about the advantages and disadvantages of each perspective.

The skeptical ontology and relativistic epistemology articulated by
Gorgias in *On Non-Existence* deny the possibility for universal truth;
and should truth in some way exist, Gorgias defines it as external to the
realm of human knowledge. Instead, Gorgias offers a nascent social constructionist view of language in which perceived realities *(ta pragmata)*
condition the generation of statements *(logoi)* about the world, making
pre-Socratic philosophical methodologies secondary intellectual endeavors to the study and use of language. If universal truth has little place in
the conduct of certain human affairs, as both Gorgias and Aristotle
contend, yet there are regulating principles that dispel anarchy (such as
ethical uses of *logos),* then these principles must have their bases in probability. The problem, however, as Gorgias explains in the *Helen,* is that
logos as a means of persuasion *(peithô)* can lead not only to communal
truths-as-probabilities but also to deceptions of opinion in the psyches
(psuchai) of rhetorical audiences. However, when *logos* is used for ethical purposes in the service of communal truths-as-probabilities, it can
help sincere orators defend those who act justly and prosecute those who
do not; and in the *Palamedes,* Gorgias offers artistic *topoi* for the invention of logical, ethical, and emotional arguments based on probability.

Viewing these Gorgianic texts as a coherent whole moves us beyond
Platonic interpretations of Gorgias's rhetorical *technê,* and this holistic
approach to *On Non-Existence,* the *Helen,* and the *Palamedes* results
in a richer understanding of the ways that forces such as *logos* serve
economic, social, and political purposes that were central to the success
of Athenian democracy in the fifth century BCE.

On Non-Existence: A Rhetorical Ontology and Epistemology

On Non-Existence details, first, the ontologically indeterminate nature
of external realities *(ta onta)* that are beyond the realm of human control; second, the effects these external realities, such as they are, have
on the human *psuchê;* and third, the problematic referential function of
logos as it applies to these external realities. And these three arguments
correlate respectively to the three theses in Gorgias's famous trilemma:
nothing exists; even if existence exists, it is inapprehensible to humans;
and even if existence is apprehensible, nevertheless it is certainly not able
to be communicated or interpreted for one's neighbors (B3.65). Throughout all three of his primary extant texts, Gorgias presents a conception

of *logos* that requires a non-essentialist ontology, and it is his rhetorical task in *On Non-Existence* to articulate this ontology in opposition to the essentialist ontologies theorized by prior pre-Socratic philosophers. Specifically, in order to establish a *technê* of *logos* and privilege it as a legitimate object of study, Gorgias must first demonstrate that realities (in the form of the first substances and foundational principles that control flux and unify difference in the cosmos) carry less impact on the human *psuchê* than had been thought by his pre-Socratic predecessors.

"Nothing exists" *(ouden estin)*, according to Gorgias, in an *essential* way—that is, neither as "existence" *(to on)* nor as "non-existence" *(to mê on)*. The term *ta onta* ("existent things" or "realities," the plural form of the singular noun *to on)*, by the late sixth century BCE, had acquired a philosophical sense and was the subject of heated pre-Socratic debates regarding existence versus non-existence and the one versus the many. In his discussion of the first thesis in the trilemma, Gorgias makes two incisive interventions: first, he argues against *both* viewing external reality as existence *and* viewing external reality as non-existence (B3.66–72), since both of these conceptions of external reality require an essentialist, totalizing ontology, and the combination of existence and non-existence is also a senseless contradiction (B3.75–76); second, Gorgias argues against *both* viewing the universe as one *(hen)* entity to be discovered through introspection *and* viewing the universe as many *(polla)* particles whose interactions require totalizing theoretical unification (B3.73–74). Finally, Gorgias concludes, "If neither non-existence exists nor existence exists nor both exist together, and if nothing is imaginable other than these, then nothing exists" (B3.76). Nothing exists (neither existence nor non-existence; neither the one nor the many), that is, in the way that prior pre-Socratic philosophers had argued, as essentialist and totalizing entities through which to explain the demythologized protoliterate world of fifth-century BCE Greece. Although Gorgias is clearly an ontological skeptic, he is not, as is often incorrectly assumed, an epistemological skeptic (see especially Hays, Crowley, Guthrie 194–200, and Kerferd 93–99).

Gorgias is an epistemological relativist, and his relativistic view of knowledge, consistent with his skeptical ontology, is apparent in his discussions of the second and third theses in his trilemma. In the second thesis, "even if anything exists, it is always unknowable and inconceivable to humans" (B3.77), Gorgias begins his arguments for a relativistic epistemology with reference to his skeptical ontology, merging the concerns of the two: If things outside the psyche do not exist, Gorgias argues, then surely they do not exist inside the psyche either (B3.77). In other words, we can not "know" in our psyches external realities as they exist (if they *exist* at all) external to our psyches. If a thing is white, we cannot know the existence of white as a property of the thing; white becomes something else, a mental representation of the whiteness of the thing, in the transformation to an intellectual state (B3.77). Then Gorgias reverses the flow of perceptual transference: "For if existent things-being-thought exist, then all things-being-thought exist, and in whatever way anyone thinks them, which is absurd." For according to Gorgias, "If one thinks about some human taking flight or chariots riding swiftly under water, neither does a human directly take flight nor do chariots ride swiftly under water" (B3.79). What we conceive through intellection, therefore, is not the same as what "exists" outside the psyche.

In the third thesis of his trilemma, "even if existence should be perceived, nevertheless it could not be communicated to another person" (B3.83), Gorgias proceeds to the problem of representing in *logos* things *(ta onta)* that might "exist," if, that is, anything exists at all. Here Gorgias argues that external realities remain external, and when perceived through human eyes and ears, these external realities become something different altogether from the realities themselves; thus, what we communicate when we speak about realities is not the realities themselves but a representation of those realities, that is, a *logos:* "For *logos* is the means by which we communicate, but *logos* is different from substances and existent things. Thus we do not communicate existent things to our neighbors; instead we communicate only *logos,* which is something other than substances" (B3.84). It is a radical departure from oral and protoliterate cultures to separate *logos* from the particular things it represents. Thus, when Gorgias says, "We do not communicate existent things to our neighbors; instead we communicate only *logos,* which is something other than material substances" (B3.84), he is in fact launching a devastating attack on the objects and methods of study common among pre-Socratic natural and metaphysical philosophers. Further, such a move is absolutely necessary for Gorgias to practice and teach an art of rhetoric, for if language re-presents (presents again, unaltered) realities in a one-to-one correspondence, as many pre-Socratics thought, then the most profitable line of inquiry is to discover the true nature of those realities through empirical or introspective philosophy, and to attempt an understanding of the *logoi* that re-present them is to pursue an artifice once removed from reality. Thus, for Gorgias to legitimate rhetoric as an intellectual endeavor in the context of pre-Socratic philosophy, he must invent a metalanguage requiring the separation of *logos* from *ta onta,* and this is the function of *On Non-Existence.*

While Gorgias does not believe in pure re-presentation, he does and must admit that "existence" evokes *logoi* or expressions of existence. The wording in *On Non-Existence* B3.85 is significant, for it shifts from using *to on* (a philosophical term) to signify external reality to using instead *to pragma,* signifying not only external reality, the term's most concrete sense, but also the deeds and circumstances of everyday communal life that are beyond our direct control and condition our social personalities. Gorgias's reference to external reality as *to pragma* ("deed" or "act," the concrete form of *praxis* that means "action" and is often used in social contexts ranging from political to business to military to poetic), a force that generates sociolinguistic *logoi,* is perhaps an early Greek articulation of a nascent social constructionist view of language. Until this passage in *On Non-Existence,* Gorgias has referred to "realities" only as *ta onta,* a philosophical term with a conceptual sense; however, when his discussion turns to the generation of *logoi,* Gorgias is no longer interested in conceptual realities since they would generate only conceptual *logoi.* Gorgias was aware, as were most fifth-century BCE Greek sophists (particularly Protagoras and the anonymous author of the *Dialexeis),* that *logoi* have a communal basis and that communal realities *(ta pragmata,* not *ta onta)* generate socially relevant discourse. Gorgias, who visited Athens as a Sicilian political ambassador (Enos 1–12), must have taken careful note of the different economic, political, social, and cultural realities throughout Greece and observed how these differing realities resulted in varying styles of argument in the specific contexts of everyday Greek life.

Having problematized an essentialist pre-Socratic conception of *logos,* Gorgias then extends the problem of representation by reversing the flow of perceptual transference, suggesting that if representation is a sociopolitical act, then *"logos* is not a representation of the external *[to ektos],* but the external becomes the signifier *[mênutikon]* of *logos"* (B3.85). This is a remarkable passage, turning prior natural and metaphysical philosophy on its ear, suggesting that reality (in this passage written as *to ektos,* the external) represents *logos;* reality, in other words, is not the most profitable intellectual pursuit because it is once removed from *logos.* Such a rhetorical move is vital to Gorgias's privileging of *logos* as a *technê* and a legitimate intellectual pursuit. For if natural philosophers do not find the study of language valuable because of its merely referential function of describing that which exists in essential ways, then Gorgias must turn this view of representation around and argue that reality serves merely the referential function of revealing *logos*. And, consequently, the art of rhetoric can be studied and is the most profitable object of study, both as a discourse in and of itself, through the metalinguistic function of language that Gorgias establishes in *On Non-Existence* B3.83 and also as a signified that is revealed through its material signifiers, through the reverse-referential function of language that Gorgias establishes in *On Non-Existence* B3.85. Moreover, Gorgias suggests that studying rhetoric as a metalanguage alone is insufficient; we must also understand its effects in the social context of its very use, and we can read meaning back into *logos*, understanding it as a signified through critical awareness of its practical effects in the public world of everyday life.

The *Encomium of Helen:* On the Negative Uses of *Peithô*

On Non-Existence is not in itself a treatise on language, much less a theory of rhetoric; instead, this text clears the ontological and epistemological grounds, consisting of realities outside of mortal control and their effects on humans, for a general theory of ways human beings move others to action, including by the agency of *logos*. Gorgias resumes this task in the *Helen* and the *Palamedes*, describing the negative uses of rhetoric as *peithô* (persuasion) in the *Helen* and the positive uses of rhetoric as a tool for inventing ethical arguments in the *Palamedes*. The opening passage of the *Helen*, with its deliberate association of *logos* and *alêtheia* (truth), raises questions regarding Gorgias's sincerity and consistency throughout the extant texts, since the skepticism and relativism in *On Non-Existence* do not appear consonant with Gorgias's desire for *alêtheia* in the *Helen*. The first sentence of the *Helen* reads: "For a city, the goodness of its citizenry is its glory, for a body it is beauty, for a soul it is wisdom, for an action it is virtue, for language *[logos]* it is truth *[alêtheia]*, and the opposites of these are a disgrace" (B11.1). This passage is so problematic outside the context of a holistic reading of the Gorgianic texts, in fact, that most scholars choose either to ignore it altogether, as John Poulakos does, or, like Thomas Cole, discount it as "a largely irrelevant introduction" to the text (76). We must keep in mind, however, that the term *alêtheia* did not develop its philosophical sense of The Truth until Plato. In most pre-Socratic and sophistic usages, *alêtheia* simply refers to sincerity of speech and is opposed to *pseudê* (lies). For Gorgias, then, *alêtheia* refers to a relative truth, which would in no way be a *pseudos* (lie), and as situations change, so, too, do the criteria for determining the truth of statements. This passage is critical to a holistic reading of the Gorgianic texts because it reinforces the interpretation of the *Helen* as a treatise on the *negative* uses of rhetoric as *peithô* (a point that many scholars like Buxton, Covino, Hays, John Poulakos, and Rosenmeyer do not recognize), for when language has no basis in communal truth, then its use may be devoid of ethics, a problem Gorgias specifically critiques in the *Palamedes*.

Having discussed the effects of external and uncontrollable realities on the human *psuchê* in *On Non-Existence* and having established early in the *Helen* a relativistic foundation of situational truth upon which to base his art of rhetoric, Gorgias then proceeds in the *Helen* to explore certain elements of *peithô* that are specifically within the control of human beings. These elements are violence *(bia)*, language *(logos)*, and physical attraction *(eros)*. For Gorgias, describing these three elements of *peithô* as human-controlled is a critical departure from the epic impulse to deify mysterious forces; in *Works and Days*, for example, Hesiod lists *Peithô, Bia, Logos,* and *Eros* as gods in the cosmic genealogy. Whereas Gorgias's task in *On Non-Existence* is to establish the possibility of a metalanguage and place *logos* at the center of intellectual pursuits, his task in the *Helen* is, in part at least, to bring *peithô* into the realm of human control, for there can be no arts *(technai)* of forces that are controlled by divine predetermination, and Gorgias must accomplish this goal by revealing and thus demystifying the workings of *peithô* (by means of human-controlled *bia, logos,* and *eros*) on the human *psuchê*.

Following a brief passage praising Helen's divine birth (daughter of Leda and Zeus) and godlike beauty, Gorgias explains four reasons not to blame Helen for her abduction to Troy: "For either by the will of Fate and the design of the gods and the decrees of Necessity did Helen do what she did *[epraxen ha epraxen]*, or she was seized by force or persuaded by words or seduced by attraction" (B11.6). The syntactic break *(epraxen ha epraxen)* between Fate, gods, and Necessity, on the one hand, and force, language, and attraction, on the other hand, is significant since the former are controlled by divine predetermination and the latter by human premeditation or "art." If, according to Gorgias, they were forces such as Fate, gods, and Necessity that caused Helen to leave Sparta, then certainly she is not to blame, "for human premeditation *[anthrôpinêi promêthiai]* is powerless to obstruct divine will *[theou prothumian]*" (B11.6). But even if *bia, logos,* or *eros* caused Helen's abduction, then she must still remain blameless. This distinction between *theou prothumian* and *anthrôpinêi promêthiai* is crucial here, since it invokes Aeschylus's *Prometheus Bound* and suggests the possibility that Gorgias considered *peithô* (by means of force, language, or attraction) to be a *technê*, albeit a potentially negative one, among the others learned by humans as a means to master their harsh world.

In *Prometheus Bound*, Hephaestus chains Prometheus to a rock at the edge of the world as punishment, by order of Zeus, for bringing fire to humans. Zeus had created the human race as an experiment, but he did not like the result, so he intended to simply let them succumb to the harsh physical conditions of the natural world, and after their inevitable demise, he would create a more favorable race of beings. But Prometheus stole from Zeus the source of fire, and through fire the human race learned a variety of arts *(technai)* that helped them master the harsh world into which Zeus had put them. Now Zeus had no way of putting an end to the human race, and his retribution for stealing art-teaching fire and giving it to humans was to chain Prometheus to a rock and have a bird eat his liver for eternity. Prometheus explains:

> But hear what troubles there were among men, how I found them witless and gave them the use of their wits and made them masters of their minds. I will tell you this, not because I would blame men, but to explain the goodwill of my gift. For men at first had eyes but saw to no purpose; they had ears but did not hear. Like the shapes of dreams they dragged through their long lives and handled all things in bewilderment and confusion. They did not know of building houses with bricks to face the sun; they did not know how to work in wood. They lived like swarming ants in holes in the ground, in the sunless caves of the earth. For them there was no secure token by which to tell winter nor the flowering spring nor the summer with its crops; all their doings were indeed without intelligent calculation until I showed them the rising of the stars, and the settings, hard to observe. And further I discovered to them numbering, pre-eminent among subtle devices, and the combining of letters [*grammatôn suntheseis*, more accurately "writing"] as a means of remembering all things, the Muses' mother, skilled in craft. (lines 441–61)

And Prometheus goes on to detail the other *technai* he made available to humans through the stolen fire: taming animals, shipbuilding, sailing, mixing medicines, telling fortunes, mapping the stars, and working metals (lines 462–506). Prometheus concludes this discourse on his role in the development of human *technai* with the following brief statement: "All arts that mortals have come from Prometheus" (line 506).

If Gorgias is invoking the Prometheus myth in the *Helen* B11.6, and I believe he is, then his use of the term *anthrôpinêi promêthiai* would synonymously invoke the *technai* or arts that Prometheus represents for humans. Gorgias, in other words, uses the term *promêthiai* to signify human-controlled forethought (that is, prelaid plans for action in the application of *technai* to anticipated yet unknown circumstances) as opposed to divine predetermination. And the human arts that Gorgias considers to be the most powerful in the service of *peithô* are *bia, logos,* and *eros.*

First, Gorgias argues that one way to influence the *psuchai* of audience members and incite them to action is through physical force *(bia)*; and, "If Helen was ravished by force and illegally abducted and unjustly violated, then it is obvious that the ravisher as the violator acted unjustly and the ravished as the violated suffered misfortune" (B11.7). Although I doubt there was an "art" of rape in the fifth century BCE, there was certainly, however, a *technê* of warfare, including forethought plans and strategies for overcoming anticipated yet unknown circumstances by means of force *(bia)*. And no citizens then were more prepared for the art of warfare than members of the political and social nobility. Helen's abductor Alexander (or Paris) was the son of Priam, king of Troy; thus, it is certain that he would have been (in the context of the myth) extensively and formally trained in a *technê* that enhanced the effectiveness of his natural strength in skirmish situations requiring physical force and violence. The role of *bia* in the ancient art of combat consisted of at least two dimensions. First, gymnastic conditioning, including wrestling and boxing, increased the naked body's power as a potentially violent force, for, as Pierre Ducrey points out, "athletics were considered basic training for war" (67). Second, weaponry enhanced the body's effective strength through prosthetic extensions of its force. Thus, as Gorgias points out, we cannot blame Helen for succumbing to physical violence (or even its potential) when it is imposed on her as a means of *peithô* by one trained in the art of *bia,* for the effect of physical force on the body and the *psuchê* can be overpowering.

Later in the *Helen,* Gorgias considers the capacity of physical attraction *(eros)* to move Helen's *psuchê* and cause her, without blame, to be abducted to Troy.[1] Here Gorgias turns again, as he did in the second thesis of his trilemma in *On Non-Existence,* to the argument that objects of sight have powerful effects on the human *psuchê,* and if it were physical attraction *(eros)* to Alexander's body *(sôma)* that moved Helen's *psuchê* and allowed her to be abducted, then surely she must not be blamed—the power of *peithô* by means of *eros* is too strong for Helen's will to withstand. Homer describes Alexander with several epithets using *aristos* (most noble in appearance) as a common thread; *aristos* in these usages emphasizes Alexander's pleasing outward appearance, which is wholly distinct from his inner character (see especially the *Iliad,* book 3). And Alexander's *aristos* drives Helen to an irrational pitch of desire. The source of *eros'* persuasive power, according to Gorgias, comes from the sensory impression, especially by means of sight, that physical beauty leaves on the human *psuchê* (see B11.16–18).

As Nicholas Gross points out, the *eros* passage in Gorgias's *Helen* draws from an ancient epic tradition, originating before Homer, that links *peithô* with *eros* (15–19, et passim). But Gorgias has in mind a more specific rhetorical purpose than had the early epic poets: Gorgias clearly focuses in this passage on visual form *(to sôma,* often opposed to *psuchê)* that when applied to the outward appearance of Alexander, Helen's abductor, can be related to an ancient art—the art of physical conditioning or gymnastics. In the context of the myth, as I have argued, Alexander, a Trojan prince, is sure to have been trained through the most rigorous gymnastic exercises, both as a required aspect of formal education and as a function of military training, enhancing the noble appearance *(aristos,* as Homer describes it in the *Iliad)* derived from his high birth; and enhancing the appearance of the *sôma* is an effective method of engaging sight in the process of *peithô* by means of *eros.*

The passage in the *Helen* that is most relevant to a Gorgianic rhetorical *technê* is B11.8–14 in which Gorgias warns his audience about the great power of *logos* in deceiving the *psuchê* and thus removes blame from Helen for her abduction to Troy. Here Gorgias argues that *logos* works in three ways to move the human *psuchê* and elicit desired physical action: first, through poetry or metrical language; second, through divine prophesies chanted in words; and third, through persuasion by means of molding false arguments.

Poetry, which Gorgias calls *"logos* with meter," elicits a range of emotions, "and in response to the condition of other people's bodies and situations in both good and ill fortune, the audience's soul evokes through the agency of words a certain emotion of its own" (B11.9). In tragic poetry, for example, beginning with dithyrambic monologues and

Aeschylean dialogues, audience members see enacted on a stage the events that cause suffering among characters, yet audiences themselves do not feel this suffering and cannot fully empathize with it until it is enhanced through the agency of metrical *logos*. Poetic situations, then, are composed of tragic events (realities) that reveal sorrowful *logoi* to dramatic characters who convey in poetic meter their sorrowful *logoi* and not the realities themselves. This double sensory experience of both tragic sight and metrical sound moves the *psuchai* of the audience to *re*live (without having *first* lived through) the tragic experiences enacted on stage. According to W. B. Stanford, the tragedians describe the strongest emotions in drama—grief and fear—"as being felt in the entrails, womb, liver, heart, midriff, lungs, or head, like a stab, or a sting, or a bite, or a fire, or a chilling frost" (21). And the tragic poets elicited these emotions from the very *psuchai* of their audiences through exaggerated visual and, more important in the context of Gorgias's *Helen,* metrical verbal representations of suffering. As Stanford points out, linguistic meter was crucial to the tragic emotive process since it could enter and influence the very rhythms of the *sôma* and *psuchê* (65–68). But *logos,* in and of itself, is not a negative force—it turns negative only when it is combined with meter to form mesmerizing poetry and is subsequently used as a *manipulative* form of *peithô,* and *logos* becomes manipulative when it deceives its audience into unsound action.

According to Gorgias, divine prophesies, like tragic drama, also move the human *psuchê* and elicit desired physical responses:

> Divine incantations chanted in words induce pleasure and drive away sorrow, for through merging with opinion, the incantation persuades and transforms the psyche through witchcraft. But the two invented arts of witchcraft and magic are failures of the psyche and faults of opinion. (*Helen* B11.10)

In this argument, Gorgias attacks another significant tradition in Greek history, the consultation of oracular prophets. Oracles such as the Pythia at Delphi, according to Dodds, were attended by priestesses who would fall into a trance, allow themselves to become "occupied" by their host deity, Apollo in the case of the Pythia, and chant mad-sounding though "divinely-inspired" riddles that were subsequently "translated" into poetic meter (*Greeks* 70–74, et passim). The resulting *logoi* of these magical frenzies, Gorgias suggests, have no meaning outside of that attributed to the riddles by the "wise men" hired to interpret them; in other words, wise men interpret the "magical" prophesies according to the *doxa* already present in their *psuchai* and not according to any meaning inherent in the jumbled *logoi* themselves. However, it is not *logos* in and of itself that creates failures of conscience and faults of opinion—it is only when magical *logoi* are chanted as divine prophesies and left to purely subjective interpretation that they move the *psuchê* to err. As Gorgias makes clear in *On Non-Existence,* "*Logos* is not a representation of the external *[to ektos]*, but the external becomes the signifier *[mênutikon]* of *logos*" (B3.85); thus, although magical prophesies take on the outward form of *logoi* (as words), nevertheless, having no connection to the external world (that is, being "divinely inspired"), they do not signify meaning but only "bear pleasure and banish pain." Thus, *peithô* by means of divine prophecies chanted in metrical language is, according to Gorgias, a negative use of *logos* as rhetoric.

The final way that *logos* moves the *psuchê* to action is through persuasion *(peithô),* which functions in many ways like poetry and prophecy. According to Gorgias, "Many people have persuaded and continue to persuade many others of many things through inventing false arguments" (B11.11). Gorgias argues that *logos* would be different if all humans regarding all subjects had perfect memory of the past, awareness of the present, and foreknowledge of the future. But since human memory and awareness are limited and foreknowledge is a luxury of the gods, then "most people regarding most subjects accept opinion as advisor to their soul. But opinion, being uncertain and unreliable, surrounds those proclaiming it with uncertain and unreliable successes" (B11.11). *Peithô* by means of *logos,* which alters opinion *(doxa)* in the *psuchê* and elicits desired physical action, according to Gorgias, forced Helen, through no fault of her own, "to believe what was said and yield to what was done" (B11.12), and so the blame must be put in its rightful place, with the persuader not the persuaded. If we recall the introduction to the *Helen* (B11.1–2) in which Gorgias opposes *alêtheia* (truth) to *pseudê* (lies), we see that any use of *logos,* especially *peithô,* that results in *pseudê logoi* (false arguments) would contradict the rhetorical ethic Gorgias articulates earlier in the text.

Gorgias continues his critique of *peithô* in the *Helen* with brief examinations of three questionable uses of *logos* as *peithô:* "In order to understand that when persuasion gives form to language it also forms the soul as it wishes, one must study" the discourses of astronomy, public debate, and philosophical argument (B11.13).

First, one must examine "the speeches of astronomers who, criticizing one opinion and replacing it with another opinion, make unbelievable and obscure things appear real to the eyes of opinion" (B11.13). Astronomy in the fifth century BCE, according to G. E. R. Lloyd, was intimately connected with what we would now call astrology. As Lloyd points out, Ptolemy, a mid-second-century CE astronomer,

> distinguishes between the two types of prediction or prognos-
> tication to be made from the study of the heavenly bodies:
> on the one hand, predictions of their movements (astronomy
> in our sense); and on the other, prediction concerning events
> on earth. Moreover, he explicitly emphasizes the conjectural
> nature and the difficulty of the latter study, criticizing the
> excessive claims made by some past and contemporary prac-
> titioners and limiting his own discussion to generalizations
> based on the supposed beneficence or maleficence of various
> heavenly bodies or their configurations. . . . Based on a be-
> lief in a connection, *sumpatheia,* between heaven and earth,
> which would be illustrated, in the first instance, by such
> uncontroversial examples as the seasons and the tides, astrol-
> ogy was usually defended (like medicine) primarily by refer-
> ence to what were claimed as its results, and as in medicine
> again, there was considerable indeterminacy in evaluating
> these. (43–44)

The *past* practitioners of astronomy to whom Ptolemy refers probably extend as far back in Greek history as Hesiod. Those practicing celestial divinations in the fifth century BCE were revered as priests and were also, not incidentally, often those called upon to "interpret" oracular riddles. But the indeterminacy of astronomical/astrological predictions raised suspicions among those, like Gorgias, who sought situated truth through the use of *logos.*

The second kind of persuasive speech we must study is "public debates requiring reasoned discourse in which one speech, written with art but not spoken with sincerity, delights and persuades a great crowd" (B11.13). Public debates and rhetorical contests were common in the sixth and fifth centuries BCE, and Gorgias was often invited to compete in them. The rhetorical goal for contest speeches among the sophists was to elicit pleasure in the audience, garnering applause that might influence the judges' favor and not *necessarily* to encourage political or ethical action. Indeed, although the participants in these public oratorical contests were often sophists who taught and practiced the most technical arts (medicine, mathematics, etc.), their rhetorical goal was not always to transmit the knowledge of their discipline to an interested audience but instead to delight a lay crowd; however, the *ethos* and *technê* of some contest orators were so powerful that at times they may have persuaded lay audiences that their *logoi,* intended as entertainment, were actually true.

The third kind of persuasive speech we must study, according to Gorgias, is "the conflicts among philosophers' arguments in which the swiftness of demonstration and judgment make the belief in any opinion changeable" (B11.13). The reference here is probably to the rapid development of natural philosophy in the sixth and fifth centuries BCE in which the speculations were often fast and loose and so contradictory as to cause suspicion. As Eric Havelock points out in "The Linguistic Task of the Pre-Socratics," the transition from orality to (whatever degree of) literacy during the centuries after Homer resulted in radical shifts in the very character of the Greek language that in turn resulted in radical shifts in the ways ancient Greeks explained their universe. Within the space of just a few centuries, Greek intellectuals turned from mythologizing the cosmos to theorizing it, and this theoretical turn generated a variety of different opinions regarding the origin and nature of the universe, religion, and the human condition.

These three contexts for *peithô*—astronomy, public debate, and philosophical argument—all demonstrate the tremendous power of *logos* to move the *psuchê* and elicit action in audiences, and the power of language in these discourses, Gorgias argues,

> has the same effect on the disposition of the soul as the prescription of drugs has on the natural constitution of bodies. For just as different drugs excrete certain humors from the body, and some end sickness while others end life, so it is with speeches: some cause grief and others pleasure, some instill fear and others steadfast courage in those who hear them, and still others drug and bewitch the psyche with a wicked kind of persuasion. (B11.14)

The discourses of astronomy, public debate, and philosophical argument, according to Gorgias, persuade audiences by false appeals to opinion in their *psuchai,* and these modes of *peithô* are consequently poor uses of language in the context of fifth-century BCE Athenian democratic politics, for democracy can only proceed on a foundation of sincerity and communal values, neither of which do astronomers nor public orators nor philosophers achieve. However, just as drugs can have positive ef-

fects on human bodies, so, too, can *logos,* and these democratic requirements of sincerity and communal values in language are precisely what
Gorgias establishes for his rhetorical *technê* in the *Palamedes.*

The *Defense of Palamedes:* The Gorgianic Art of Rhetoric

Although Palamedes, the narrator of this text, is a mythical character,
Gorgias's very choice of mythic figure reveals a concern for rhetorical
invention as a technical art: Palamedes is said to have significantly benefited Greece and her citizens, as Gorgias tells us, by *inventing* protec-
tive armor, written laws, the alphabet, measures and weights, and number (B11a.30). And early in the *Palamedes,* following a brief introduction
to the mythic rhetorical situation of Odysseus's charge of treason against
Palamedes, Gorgias articulates (through the mouthpiece of Palamedes)
a concern specifically for the invention of arguments in judicial cases:

> For an accusation that is unsupported by proof causes con-
> fusion in court. And due to the present confusion [caused by
> Odysseus's unsupported accusation], I am, of course, at a loss
> for words, unless I can invent *[mathô]* some defense from the
> truth *[alêtheia]* itself and the present necessity *[anankê].*
> (B11a.4)

When confronted with unsupported allegations, according to Gorgias,
the orator must invent a defense from the intersection of relatively consistent truths and the ever changing variables of each unique rhetorical
situation; and in the *Palamedes,* Gorgias suggests that arguments regarding honor and dishonor must not partake of *doxa* but instead should
partake of *alêtheia* in conjunction with the present necessity *(anagkê).*
The invention of arguments thus takes a central role in the Gorgianic
art of rhetoric. As the text of the *Palamedes* proceeds, Gorgias exemplifies a topical method for inventing logical, ethical, and, when necessary, emotional arguments from probability *(eikos);* and these *topoi,*
though presented in the narrative context of the Palamedes myth, are
similar in many ways to the *topoi* for the invention of logical, ethical,
and emotional arguments from probability described by Aristotle in
the *Rhetoric.*[2]

A number of the *topoi* for logical arguments from probability regarding motive and capability that Gorgias demonstrates in the *Palamedes* appear as forensic *topoi* for past-fact arguments over a century
later in Aristotle's *Rhetoric.* According to Aristotle:

> Whether some action has or has not taken place should be
> considered on the basis of the following *[topoi]*. First, if what
> is naturally less likely to have happened [happened], what is
> more so should also have happened. And if what usually
> occurs after something else has happened [happened], the
> previous event has also happened. . . . (2.19.16–17)

In the *Palamedes*, Gorgias exemplifies inventional *topoi* similar to
Aristotle's, suggesting that the capability to commit treason requires a
succession of probable occurrences: the genesis of the supposed deed in
speech/discussion *(logos)*, its security through a sworn pledge, hostages,
or monetary exchange, and its final success in not being detected by
guards or loyal citizens. Gorgias supplies for each requirement a set of
inventional *topoi* (literally, places) from which to invent *(mathein)* arguments from probability *(eikos)* about capability. Treason, for example,
must occur through language, but Palamedes does not speak any language other than Greek so the probability does not exist that Palamedes
committed treason (B11a.6–7). Further, Gorgias suggests that in the
event of treason and monetary exchange, it is most likely that Palamedes
would have been detected re-entering Odysseus's military camp with the
barbarian payoff. But since no such thing was detected, it is not probable that the act of treason was committed at all (B11a.12).

Turning his inventional efforts of logical arguments toward motive,
Aristotle continues:

> And if a person had the capacity and the will [to do some-
> thing], he has done it; for all act when ability to do so coin-
> cides with desire; for nothing hinders them. Further, if some-
> one had the will to do something and no external agency
> hindered him, [then he acted], and if he had the ability and
> was angry, and if he had the ability and longed for something
> [, then he acted]; for usually people do what they long to do
> if they can, the bad through lack of self-control, the good
> because they desire good things. And if something was go-
> ing to happen and someone was going to do it, [then it oc-
> curred]; for it is probable that one who was going to do some-
> thing also did it. (*Rhetoric* 2.19.18–21)

In the *Palamedes*, Gorgias exemplifies inventional *topoi* for inventing
arguments from probability regarding motive, and these *topoi* are in
many ways similar to Aristotle's. According to Gorgias, motive requires

potential advantage—social status, wealth, honor, security—but there would have been no advantage for Palamedes to commit treason. Gorgias suggests, for example, that even if "no external agency hindered him," Palamedes would not have motive to commit treason, since no Greek wishes for social power among barbarians (B11a.13) who would not trust a Greek traitor anyway (B11a.13–14). Further, monetary gain would be motive to commit treason, but Palamedes has no need of money; and men are motivated to act for desire of honor, but Palamedes points out that no honor can come from betraying one's friends and family (B11a.16–18). The only significant difference between Aristotle's logical *topoi* and Gorgias's logical *topoi* is that Aristotle's are acontextual while Gorgias places his in the narrative context of the Palamedes myth.

Having demonstrated logically by means of probability that Palamedes had neither the capacity nor motive to commit treason, Gorgias then turns from *logos* to *ethos* and exemplifies *topoi* for the invention of arguments regarding the characters of the accuser and the accused in much the same way that Aristotle does.[3] According to Aristotle:

> Since rhetoric is concerned with making a judgment, . . . it is necessary not only to look to the argument, that it may be demonstrative and persuasive, but also [for the speaker] to construct a view of himself as a certain kind of person and to prepare the judge. (*Rhetoric* 2.1.2)

Aristotle continues, "There are three reasons why speakers themselves are persuasive; for there are three things we trust other than logical demonstrations. These are practical wisdom *[phronêsis]* and virtue *[aretê]* and good will *[eunoia]*" (2.1.5). Regarding the character of the accuser, in this case Odysseus, Gorgias writes (and Palamedes speaks), "It is appropriate to understand such a man who says such things as worthless by means of worthlessness" (B11a.22), and Palamedes continues, "So then, most reckless of all humans, trusting in opinion (a most untrustworthy thing), not understanding the truth, do you recklessly seek the death penalty for another man?" (B11a.24). Gorgias thinks little of *doxa* in the *Palamedes* as a means to persuade audiences, in this instance judges in a court case, to potentially unethical action (a position similar to the one he takes in the *Helen* B11.8–14). Throughout this section of the text, Gorgias's Palamedes implies that Odysseus lacks practical wisdom, virtue, and goodwill in his attempt to destroy Palamedes based on *doxa* and not *alêtheia* (B11a.22–26), yet he refuses to develop these arguments at length, saying:

> Although I would be quite able to make a countercharge
> against the many crimes, both past and recent, that you have
> committed, I do not wish to do so; for I do not wish to be
> acquitted from this accusation by reference to your evil deeds
> but rather by reference to my own virtuous deeds. (B11a.27)

Turning, then, to his own character, Palamedes suggests that self-praise is "not appropriate for one who has not been accused of a crime, but it is proper for one who has been accused" (B11a.28), and Gorgias exemplifies in this section a few different *topoi* for praising the good character (that is, the practical wisdom, virtue, and goodwill) of the accused in any court case. Palamedes reminds the judges, for example, that his many inventions, by means of practical wisdom, have benefited the very Greeks he is accused of betraying:

> For who else would have made human existence self-suffi-
> cient rather than helpless and adorned rather than offensive
> by inventing the most protective armor, and written laws, the
> guardians of justice, and the alphabet, the instrument of
> memory, and measures and weights, the successful mediation
> of commercial exchange, and number, the guardians of prop-
> erty, and the strongest beacons and the fastest messengers,
> and draughts, the harmless game of leisure. (B11a.30)

And as a consequence, these virtuous endeavors to improve the lives of Greeks signify that Palamedes because of his virtue also abstains completely from "shameful and evil activities" (B11a.31). Finally, Palamedes demonstrates his goodwill, reminding the jury that he is "harmless to the elderly, not useless to the youthful, not jealous of the prosperous, but compassionate toward the misfortunate" (B11a.32). This method of argument from the character of the accused in the *Palamedes* is strikingly similar to the method suggested in Aristotle's rhetorical *technê,* and it is likely that the *topoi* Gorgias demonstrates in this text were in common use well before Aristotle described them.

Having discussed logical and ethical appeals in legal rhetoric, Gorgias turns finally to emotional appeals or *pathos,* which both Gorgias and Aristotle consider to belong last in the structure of forensic discourse (see Aristotle, *Rhetoric* 3.19.1; in the *Palamedes,* Gorgias simply addresses *pathos* last). According to Aristotle, "[There is persuasion] through the hearers when they are led to feel emotion *[pathos]* by the speech; for we do not give the same judgment when grieved or rejoicing or when being friendly [or] hostile" (1.2.5). Like Aristotle, Gorgias believes that emotional appeals are inferior to logical and ethical arguments because emotional appeals assume a lack of rhetorical capacity on the part of the audience:

> Lamentation and sorrowful prayers and the intercession of friends are effective when a judgment is made before a crowd, but among you, who are the foremost of the Greeks and renown citizens, there is no need to persuade such ones as you with the aid of friends and sorrowful prayers and lamentations; professing truth and not deceiving you, I must refute this accusation by means of the clearest justice. (B11a.33)

Although Gorgias does not neglect *pathos* entirely, he clearly privileges logical and ethical arguments from probability over those designed to dispose juries toward a particular judgment regardless of the *alêtheia* at hand. Regarding the jury, Gorgias writes:

> You must neither turn your attention more to arguments than to actions, nor prejudge the motives of my defense, nor consider that a short amount of time results in a wiser judgment than a long time, nor believe in false accusations more than the assurance of experience. (B11a.34)

Gorgias continues:

> If, through arguments, the truth of actions could become clear and apparent to hearers, your judgment would now be easy based upon what has been said. But since truth does not have control over these arguments, guard my body, strive for a longer amount of time, and derive your judgment from truth. (B11a.35)

Logoi alone, Gorgias argues in *On Non-Existence,* are often inaccurate representations of real events, and the most ethical judgment, returning to the *Palamedes,* is one that looks beyond unreliable present words to prior actions, that is, the virtuous actions of the accused Palamedes that contradict the unjust accusation of Odysseus.

In the *Nicomachean Ethics,* Aristotle defines a *technê* as a "reasoned habit of mind in making" (4.4.1–6; in Kennedy 288–89). The Gorgianic texts that have survived the past two-and-a-half millennia have characteristics of what I call pedagogical paradigm speeches designed specifically to develop in Gorgias's students a "reasoned habit of mind in making" logical, ethical, and, if necessary, emotional arguments from probability. In rhetorical situations requiring deliberation and judgment regarding human actions, according to Gorgias and Aristotle, the rhetor invents discourse based on probability using *topoi* appropriate to the requirements of the moment, and both the extant Gorgianic texts and Aristotle's *Rhetoric* provide students with a theory and practice of topical invention. Although Gorgias probably did have students memorize his speeches (for which he was criticized by Plato and Aristotle), it was not so that they would repeat the same *logoi* in every situation but rather so that they might have memorized examples of different inventional *topoi* available to them for the various situations they might encounter in their own professional oratorical lives. Finally, considering the many significant theoretical and pragmatic parallels between Aristotle's *Rhetoric* and the extant Gorgianic texts (especially the *Palamedes*), it would be remarkable to consider one a *technê* and not the other, regardless of what Plato thought; indeed, Plato probably would have considered Aristotle's rhetorical theory and practice, due to its focus on argument from probability, to be inartistic—*atechnê*.

As I have argued throughout this chapter, *On Non-Existence* theorizes the impact that external realities *(ta onta)* beyond human control have on the human *psuchê*, the *Helen* explores the negative impact that human-controlled forces *(promêthiai)* can have on the human *psuchê*, and the *Palamedes* demonstrates a variety of inventional *topoi* that can encourage desired ethical actions in audiences. In this holistic reading of Gorgias's extant texts, I argue against interpretations of Gorgianic rhetoric that locate its foundations in skeptical notions of opinion *(doxa)*, persuasion *(peithô)*, and deception *(apatê)*, offering instead a relativistic interpretation locating the bases of Gorgianic doctrines in communal *alêtheia* and ethics.

Part Two

Neosophistic Appropriation

3
Neosophistic Rhetorical Theory

The goal of historical interpretation in scholarship on the sophists is to recover, as best we can, the doctrines professed by these traveling teachers of fifth-century BCE Greece. Given this goal of recovery, writers practicing historical interpretation operate between two points on a continuum: attempting to put aside the modern anachronistic frameworks that they know were not available to the sophists, although they can never put all of them aside, or acknowledging their own conceptual starting points in a theoretical confession and proceeding with caution. The critical methodologies used in historical interpretation are intended to result in complete pictures of ancient events and doctrines. Throughout the first two chapters of *Gorgias and the New Sophistic Rhetoric,* I engage in historical interpretation, attempting to recover Gorgias's art of rhetoric as he might have described it to his contemporaries, putting aside anachronistic, neoplatonic frameworks (at least those of which I am conscious) and reading the extant Gorgianic texts holistically.

However, as I argue in the Introduction, neosophistic appropriation has different goals and methods from historical interpretation. Thus, as we begin part two of this book, it is important to examine the specific goals of neosophistic rhetoric and the methods neosophists use to achieve them. Neosophists have little interest in doing history for its own sake, and they are not concerned with constructing complete pictures of the sophists and their doctrines. Instead, neosophists "mine" sophistic doctrines and historical interpretations of these doctrines for theories and methods that contribute solutions to problems in contemporary rhetoric. Once rediscovered, these ancient theories and methods are transported from their original historical contexts into modern contexts, and they are remolded in ways that the exigencies of the original historical contexts might not have suggested or even allowed. The results are *neo-doctrines* that are no longer the same as their respective classical doctrines, yet through all of their adaptations and appropriations, the neo-doctrines still retain traces of their origins.

A certain view of historiography goes along (or *should* go along) with the neosophistic goal of appropriation and methods of mining and transporting doctrines, a view based on sophistic principles. First, let me paraphrase Gorgias in a conscious *appropriation,* invoking his famous trilemma in the service of historiography: historical reality does not exist in any *essential* form; even if historical reality exists, historians can not know it except through the process of interpretation; even if historians can know historical reality as it exists external to interpretation, they cannot convey that historical reality to another person, since language, like reality, is always interpreted. In "Toward a Sophistic Historiography" Jarratt also argues that we should approach the sophists through historical methodologies derived from their own thought, and she looks "to the works of the sophists themselves as a kind of creative analog for a particular kind of historical practice" (264).[1] The "practice of sophistic historiography entails," according to Jarratt,

1. a redefinition and consequent expansion of the materials and subject matters of rhetorical history, resulting in what today would be styled multidisciplinary—historical investigations on the margins of traditionally conceived disciplines;
2. the denial of progressive continuity: a conscious attempt to disrupt the metaphor of a complete and full chain of events with a *telos* in the revival of rhetoric in the twentieth century; and,
3. the employment of two pre-logical language *technê,* antithesis and parataxis, creating narratives distinguished by multiple or open causality, the indeterminacies of which are then resolved through the self-conscious use of probable arguments. (264)

Multiple perspectives, ruptured narratives, competing arguments—these are the basic premises of sophistic historiography upon which much neosophistic rhetorical appropriation is based.

But what are the consequences of this historiography? If our goal is not to reconstruct ancient doctrines in their entirety but to appropriate only the useful doctrines, to transport them from one context to another, what happens to the doctrines themselves? Edward Said offers an account of how theories *travel,* and this account also explains the process of appropriation that has taken place in neosophistic studies. Said writes:

> Like people and schools of criticism, ideas and theories travel—from person to person, from situation to situation, from one period to another. Cultural and intellectual life are usually nourished and often sustained by this circulation of ideas, and whether it takes the form of acknowledged or unconscious influence, creative borrowing, or wholesale appropriation, the movement of ideas and theories from one place to another is both a fact of life and a usefully enabling condition of intellectual activity. Having said that, however, one should go on to specify the kinds of movement that are possible, in order to ask whether by virtue of having moved from one place in time to another an idea or a theory gains or loses in strength, and whether a theory in one historical period and national culture becomes altogether different for another period or situation. . . . Such movement into a new environment is never unimpeded. It necessarily involves processes of representation and institutionalization different from those at the point of origin. This complicates any account of the transplantation, transference, circulation, and commerce of theories and ideas. (226)

During the 1970s, 1980s, and 1990s, sophistic rhetoric *traveled:* it was transported from the fifth century BCE into twentieth century CE rhetorical theory and composition studies, and this process of transportation enabled new "intellectual activities."[2] Of course, it would be naïve to suggest that sophistic doctrines have traveled without experiencing the pressures and constraints of a new time and place; indeed, they *have,* and it will be one task of this chapter to explore some of these new pressures and constraints, these new "processes of representation and institutionalization."

Yet are we able to identify any consistent characteristics of the process that traveling theories undergo? Said believes we are:

> There is . . . a discernible and recurrent pattern to the movement itself, three or four stages common to the way any theory or idea travels. First, there is a point of origin, or what

seems like one, a set of initial circumstances in which the idea came to birth or entered discourse. Second, there is a distance traversed, a passage through the pressure of various contexts as the idea moves from an earlier point to another time and place where it will come into a new prominence. Third, there is a set of conditions—call them conditions of acceptance or, as an inevitable part of acceptance, resistances—which then confronts the transplanted theory or idea, making possible its introduction or toleration, however alien it might appear to be. Fourth, the now fully (or partly) accommodated (or incorporated) idea is to some extent transformed by its new uses, its new position in a new time and place. (226–27)

A genealogy of neosophistic rhetoric's travels is easy to construct based on Said's four stages. First, although many of the ideas that certain sophists professed were in current circulation centuries before them (the notion of *kairos,* for example, can be traced back to Hesiod), the democratic political climate of the fifth century BCE was fertile ground for the development and extension of these ideas into the rhetorical arts. Thus, the "point of origin" for the doctrines most often appropriated by neosophists is (constructed or represented as) fifth-century BCE sophistic rhetoric. Second, sophistic doctrines have traveled along a path riddled with the pressures of Platonic misrepresentations, epistemological realisms, and current-traditional rhetorics. Third, marked by the rise of poststructuralist rhetorics and the writing-process movement in composition, a new set of conditions emerged during the latter half of the twentieth century, conditions that enabled the critique of Plato's hegemony, foundational epistemologies, and realist rhetorics. Fourth, because of the transformations sophistic rhetoric has undergone in the process of traveling from the fifth century BCE to the twentieth and twenty-first centuries CE, what we now call neosophistic rhetoric bears only some resemblance to its original namesake.

In this chapter, I explore three theoretical and pedagogical sites where neosophists appropriate sophistic doctrines to solve contemporary problems in composition and rhetorical studies: epistemic relativism and the ethics of rhetoric, poststructuralism and the politics of public discourse, and feminist and third sophistics. Of course, any attempt to categorize positions within a more general movement such as the revival of sophistry is necessarily rife with difficulties. It involves the imposition of structure where structure does not inherently reside; it seeks fundamental differences where similarities abound. I am conscious that other neosophists would devise other schemes; however, since any critical act is an act of structural imposition, I proceed, though with caution.

Epistemic Relativism and the Ethics of Rhetoric

Daniel J. Royer argues that "Epistemic rhetoric is the culmination of many influences that ultimately sink their roots in the philosophies of Cassirer and Kant" (287). While Cassirer, Kant, and others have left their marks on contemporary theories of rhetoric as epistemic, Royer neglects perhaps their most profound sources of inspiration—the older sophists and Gorgias in particular. But why turn to the sophists as predecessors? In 1978, Michael C. Leff explained, "Since the epistemic view of rhetoric is revolutionary in the context of modern thought, we lack a stable vocabulary in which to define it" ("In Search" 77), and the turn toward the sophists helped solve this problem of articulation. Two seminal articles in the history of the discussion of rhetoric as epistemic invoke the sophists in general and Gorgias in particular as epistemological predecessors for this (then) new way of viewing the role of language in the formation of human knowledge: Robert L. Scott's "On Viewing Rhetoric as Epistemic" and Leff's "In Search of Ariadne's Thread."

Scott provides the first full articulation of epistemic rhetorical theory. In this landmark essay, Scott uses arguments from Toulmin, Gorgias, and Protagoras to combat traditional Platonic and analytical conceptions of knowledge and truth that had stifled rhetorical theory in the early twentieth century. Early in the essay, Scott invokes a question from Plato's *Gorgias,* a question that is at the center of rhetorical epistemology: Socrates asks Gorgias, "Shall we, then, assume two kinds of persuasion, the one producing belief without certainty, the other knowledge?" (10; recall my critique of this opposition in chapter 1). According to Scott, a Platonic belief in the existence of truth and knowledge as analytically demonstrable and prior to experience leads logically to a belief in only two modes of discourse: "a neutral presenting of data among equals and a persuasive leading of inferiors by the capable" (10). But an epistemic (and sophistic) belief in the historical and empirical contingency of truth recovers rhetoric as a mode of thought. Sophistic/epistemic rhetoric creates truth through "cooperative critical inquiry" (13–14), and by reference to "generally accepted social norms, experience, or even matters of faith," rhetoric helps humans resolve "the contingencies in which [they] find themselves" (12).

Like Gorgias before him, Scott contends:

> Truth is not prior and immutable but is contingent. Insofar
> as we can say that there is truth in human affairs, it is in time;
> it can be the result of a process of interaction at a given mo-
> ment. Thus rhetoric may be viewed not as a matter of giving
> effectiveness to truth but of *creating truth*. (13, my emphasis)

In order to emphasize that his argument is historically situated, Scott interprets Gorgias's *On Non-Existence* "as an attempt to show that man
can be certain of no absolute standard. We may be aware of the attributes
of our experiences, but there is no way for us to recognize any attribute
which is *essential* among experiences" (15, my emphasis). Scott's sophis-
tic/epistemic model of rhetoric suggests that humans interact dialectically with each other and with their material conditions, thereby creating rhetorical knowledge. When viewed in this way, Scott suggests,
rhetoric "is a way of knowing; it is epistemic" (17), and the sophistic
doctrines of Gorgias provide the historical traditions that frame Scott's
discussion.

Leff reinforces and extends many of Scott's prior conclusions. In his
review of speech communication scholarship from 1976 to 1977, Leff
suggests that "there appears to be an emerging consensus in support of
Scott's view that rhetoric is epistemic" (75), and "the connection between
rhetoric and knowing has had an exhilarating effect on rhetoricians who
have suffered through long years of abuse from positivists, idealists,
intuitionists, and other pure thinkers who occupy the higher levels of
the academic totem pole" (77). Leff identifies four senses in which rhetoric is epistemic, and he lists them from "weakest" to "boldest":

1. Rhetoric is epistemic because it allows us to know how
   particular objects and events relate to fixed, abstract principles.
2. Rhetoric is epistemic because it represents an active, social form of thinking that allows us to gain knowledge
   both of particulars and of principles in respect to practical matters.
3. Rhetoric is epistemic since it can serve a metalogical function that helps us to secure knowledge of the first principles of theoretical disciplines.
4. Rhetoric is epistemic since knowledge itself is a rhetorical
   construct. (78)

Leff derives his fourth version of epistemic rhetoric—in which we "view epistemology as rhetorical" (82)—from Gorgias and Kenneth Burke, and it is only this "bold" version that concerns me here. Leff points out that "knowledge itself is a rhetorical construct," and he identifies two claims that are characteristic of this view: (1) "the symbolic and normative aspects of knowledge are prior to the objective and mechanical" and (2) "the rhetorical function is the dominant aspect of the symbolic process" (83). Leff explains the imbrication of rhetoric and epistemology:

> Denying the possibility of certain and immutable knowledge, Gorgias holds that our view of reality is based exclusively on opinion. We know what we know on the basis of encounters with actual situations as they are defined by the perceptual screen of language. The antithetical power of language creates the illusion of reality by framing our responses in terms of simple oppositions. Language provides concrete models and anti-models that allow us to make sense of the world. Furthermore, as its antithetical structure suggests, language itself operates through conflict and is therefore fundamentally persuasive in character. Consequently, the rhetor commands the whole field of epistemology. (84)

According to Leff, linguistic, cultural, and material forces operate dialectically to create knowledge, leading to the view that knowledge itself is rhetorical, and this language/culture/reality dialectic was first theorized by the sophist Gorgias during the fifth century BCE. Leff concludes with the following statement that emphasizes the radical nature of this epistemic turn to the sophists:

> Surely, it is significant that the thinking of Gorgias, rather than Plato or Aristotle, provided the point of entry into antiquity. Even in the absence of other evidence, this fact should alert us to the profound changes occasioned by granting rhetoric an epistemic status. (84)

Yet, just as Plato and Aristotle accused the sophists of unethical practices (that is, practices that were based on their epistemological relativism), so, too, does epistemic relativism fall prey to such accusations from contemporary rhetorical theorists. Scott and Leff anticipate charges against epistemic ethics and defend this relativistic rhetoric, arguing that foundational rhetorics do not require human responsibility in the process of ethical decision making. According to Scott, epistemic truth (or relativist truth) "does not exist prior to but in the working out of its own expression. . . . Inaction, failure to take on the burden of participating in the development of contingent truth, ought to be considered ethical failure" (16). Scott explains:

> If one can act with certainty of truth then any effects of that action can be viewed as inevitable, that is, determined by the principles for which the individual is simply the instrument; the individual acting is not responsible for the pain, for example, that his actions may bring to himself or to others. The man who views himself as the instrument of the state, or of history, or of certain truth of any sort puts himself beyond ethical demands, for he says, in effect, "It is not I who am responsible."
>
> On the contrary, one who acts without certainty must embrace the responsibility for making his acts the best possible. He must recognize the conflicts of the circumstances that he is in, maximizing the potential good and accepting responsibility for the inevitable harm. If the person acts in circumstances in which harm is not an ever-present potential, then he is not confronted by ethical questions. . . . To act with intentions for good consequences, but to accept the responsibilities for all the consequences insofar as they can be known is part of what being ethical must mean. (16–17)

For Scott and Leff, the very precondition for ethical behavior is contingency, and since sophistic and epistemic rhetorics presume a universe of contingencies, it is only within these ancient and modern relativistic approaches to the nature and function of discourse that ethics can emerge.

Epistemic rhetoric, then, has its deepest and most significant roots in the rhetorical theories of the ancient sophists and of Gorgias in particular. Although only a few contemporary proponents of rhetoric as epistemic self-consciously invoke their pre-Platonic theoretical predecessors, I believe that the older sophists are present at the center or on the margins (overtly or covertly) in every instance of metadiscourse about epistemic rhetoric. James S. Baumlin sees tremendous influence from the sophists Gorgias and Protagoras in contemporary epistemic rhetoric, pointing out that James A. Berlin's descriptions of the so-called new rhetoric are "suggestively similar" to the ancient sophistic discussions of contingent reality and relative truth. Baumlin concludes, "I am puzzled that it should even be called the 'new' rhetoric, since the epistemology and principles of organic form underlying it were fully developed many centuries ago in the rhetorical theories of Gorgias, Protagoras, and Isocrates" (179).

While Scott and Leff make sweeping appropriations of sophistic epistemologies in the service of articulating a new epistemic rhetoric, other neosophists have made specific appropriations of one sophistic doctrine, *kairos* (seizing the opportune moment), in order to develop our ideas of epistemic rhetoric, writing across the curriculum, and rhetorical invention. As I argued in chapter 1, the sophists, Gorgias in particular, formulated rhetorical strategies to exploit the qualitative conception of time known as *kairos*. As a social practice, *kairos* functions best in the context of a contingent world view since universal truth does not know space or time. And as a rhetorical strategy, exploiting *kairos* is most effective within an epistemic view of discourse since, as I have said, any time is the right time when one possesses truth, but when nothing is certain, then time is of the essence. Although Plato included a conception of *kairos* in his own philosophical rhetoric, its purpose lies only in the adaptation of universal truth to various audiences. But a sophistic and epistemic view of *kairos* elevates its function to the very construction of knowledge in discourse, and it is this sophistic and epistemic view of *kairos* that has been appropriated by neosophists in the service of epistemic rhetoric, writing across the curriculum, and rhetorical invention.

In "Decorum, *Kairos,* and the 'New' Rhetoric," for example, Baumlin argues that "through *kairos,* the writer or speaker recognizes the mutability of the world and the power that the word of *logos* plays in constituting reality; and decorum, united with *kairos,* becomes the principle of adapting all elements of discourse to a world of change" (177). Baumlin continues:

> Sophistic rhetoric, therefore, and particularly the concept of *kairos,* persists as a pre-Socratic legacy to all classically-based theories of rhetoric: to Aristotle and Cicero, to Puttenham and Bacon, and certainly to modern man, the world is a world of contradiction, where an act is effective now and ineffective later, a word true under one circumstance and false under another. The observance of *kairos* becomes above all an interpretation of mutable, contingent, temporal nature, giving the speaker or writer what amounts to creative control over the world he lives in and presents, by words, to others.

> In fact *kairos* . . . offers a classically-based epistemology for
> modern rhetoric—a rhetoric that recognizes the contingent
> nature of reality and the way man constitutes his world
> through language. (180–81)

Based on his observation of affinities between ancient sophistic doctrines
of *kairos* and recent articulations of epistemic rhetoric, Baumlin finally
urges an appropriative return "to *kairos* as the foundation of modern
discourse" (179).

James L. Kinneavy presents a complex view of *kairos* in classical
rhetoric, and he applies this complex conception of "right timing" or
"proper measure" (85) to modern composition studies, arguing specifically for its inclusion among theories informing writing across the curriculum. According to Kinneavy, the ancient concept of *kairos* partici-
pates in at least five dimensions—ethical, epistemological, rhetorical,
aesthetic, and civic—of human social activity. Although Kinneavy warns
us that the "problem in applying this rich concept to college composition is the danger of losing some of its essential complexity," he nevertheless admits that "the attempt should be worthwhile. Indeed, it may
lend a unity to several separate movements" (93). Kinneavy continues:

> What is required, if we are to be faithful to our historical
> analysis, is to devise a college composition program that will
> have ethical, epistemological, rhetorical, aesthetic, and po-
> litical dimensions involving something like a notion of con-
> temporary practical relevance to the young women and men
> of today. (93–94)

For Kinneavy, *kairos* has much to do with decision making, and there
is no time in most person's lives more packed with important decisions
than the time spent in college, and university writing programs can aid
students, exploiting the various dimensions of *kairos,* in making sound
foundational decisions (94).

Kinneavy urges composition teachers to turn from their present
concentration on texts to a more pragmatic concentration on situational
contexts, a modern conception of *kairos* that has its roots in sophistic
epistemologies. The situational contexts to which Kinneavy refers are
based on disciplinary rhetoric or writing across the curriculum (95–98).
Yet, a composition program based on *kairos* must also include an ethical dimension; thus, at least part of the writing in this program must
explore the "values implicit in the discipline" under scrutiny and the

"ethical concerns" of each student's "personal interests and career choices" (98). Further, this *kairos* writing program must also require students to place the situational context and ethical values implicit in their disciplinary and career choices into a broader social context or historical consciousness. In so doing, the writing program moves in the direction of civic education, requiring "some writing by the students on the political issues relevant to their own disciplines and on the political scene generally" (99). But Kinneavy does not believe that these ethical and political dimensions of *kairos* are enough of a base for a writing program; it must also develop rhetorical skills in its students.

> The politics, the ethics, and the rhetoric of a profession ought to be a part of the curriculum of any discipline. And the rhetoric of the discipline means the ability to address the populace in persuasive language that will be listened to. And this persuasive language will often have to be intensive, even impassioned, audience based and biased, and stylistically appropriate to a given subculture. (102)

Thus, *kairos,* in all of its complex dimensions, provides a sound foundation (though certainly not a *foundational* foundation) upon which to build modern writing programs, ones that incorporate ethical, political, and rhetorical issues into a comprehensive curriculum.

In their composition textbook *Ancient Rhetorics for Contemporary Students* (second edition), Sharon Crowley and Debra Hawhee appropriate the ancient doctrine of *kairos* to solve a more narrowly focused problem than Kinneavy's sweeping reform of contemporary writing programs. Crowley and Hawhee appropriate *kairos* to explore and illuminate issues specific to epistemic rhetorical invention. Following a brief explanation of the sophistic conception of the right time and place, Crowley and Hawhee offer composition students a useful heuristic to help them think about *kairos* as a form of invention. "Remembering that *kairos* is not only a concept of time but also of space, a rhetor concerned about *kairos* can explore questions such as these":

1. Does the issue have a sense of urgency right now, or do I need to show its urgency or make it relevant to the present?
2. What arguments seem to be advantageous with what groups at this point in time?
3. What lines of argument might be inappropriate considering the prevailing needs and values of the audience?

4. What other issues are bound up with discourse about this particular issue right now, in this place and in this community? Why?
5. What are the particular power dynamics at work in the issue? Who has power? Who doesn't?
6. What venues give voices to which sides of the issues? Does one group or another seem to be in a better position from which to argue? Why?
7. Does one group seem to have a louder voice than the others? Why is this so? (36–37)

Crowley and Hawhee conclude, "A rhetor attuned to *kairos* should consider a particular issue as a set of distinct political pressures, personal investments, and values, all of which produce different arguments about an issue" (42). As such, the ancient conception of *kairos* is extremely useful for contemporary students, especially in the kind of argumentative academic writing that occurs in composition classes as well as throughout the undergraduate curriculum.

The ancient sophists, Gorgias and Protagoras in particular, and the doctrine of *kairos* have proven to be useful and fruitful resources for solving modern problems relating to the articulation of epistemic rhetoric, the development of writing programs, and the practice of rhetorical invention. Sophistic doctrines have also been useful in the development of poststructuralist and pragmatist rhetorics of public discourse.

Poststructuralism, Pragmatism, and Public Discourse

While the neosophists discussed in the previous section focused their efforts exclusively on *rhetoric,* ancient and modern, this next group of neosophists finds affinities between sophistic *rhetorical* traditions and modern *philosophical* traditions, especially poststructuralism and pragmatism, appropriating not only the rhetorical doctrines of the sophists but also the doctrines of modern philosophers in the service of re-visioning composition and rhetorical studies as politicized public discourse.

Crowley, one of the first scholars to link poststructuralism and sophistry, argues that Gorgias's premetaphysical rhetoric and Derrida's critique of metaphysical presence both offer alternatives to the stifling epistemologies and methodologies characteristic of current-traditional rhetoric. In "Of Gorgias and Grammatology," Crowley suggests that the "assumption, borrowed from the metaphysics of presence, that language somehow represents or describes a reality external to it, had, until quite recently, kept rhetoricians from thinking about language in productive ways." Instead, Crowley asserts, the "art of rhetoric is not an art of presence, of seeking truth," but "an art of the use of language, of the pragmatics of discourse. . . . Even though the metaphysics of presence has dominated Western thought, its representation theory of language is not very useful for rhetorical theory or for the study and teaching of language in general and writing in particular" (279). Crowley laments that

> writing is taught in schools not as a means of tapping the power and charm of the word but as a less-than-satisfactory representation of speech. Students are taught to use writing in good metaphysical style: don't let the written words get between the ideas and the reader; words should be transparent, like glass. (284)

According to Crowley, the most important contributions that Gorgias makes to a theory, practice, and pedagogy of writing, one that avoids the pitfalls of what Derrida later called the metaphysics of presence, are, first, that language is not connected naturally to truth and reality, and second, that a writer's attention is always directed toward the effects words have on an audience (280–82). Crowley concludes with two consequences of the Gorgianic and Derridean critiques of presence: "First, we should try to implant in our students a Gorgianic respect for the power and magic of language," and second, "teachers of composition should start thinking of writing not as a handmaiden of speech but as a powerful instrument of *logos*" (284). Crowley thus offers Gorgias's premetaphysical sophistry and Derrida's poststructuralist neosophistry as an antidote to the stifling rigidity of current-traditional rhetoric.

In *Plato, Derrida, and Writing,* Jasper Neel negotiates an aporia between Plato's foundational dialectics and Derrida's negative deconstruction, both *philosophical* (not rhetorical) positions from which Neel attempts to "save" writing (xi), and within this aporia he finds "strong discourse" or discourse that is able to withstand the scrutiny of public contest. Here Neel offers "sophistry as the mode of operating in a post-Platonic, poststructuralist world," and his "purpose is to attempt to clear a place in intellectual history where the act of writing is neither shameful (as Plato would have it) nor philosophical (as Derrida would have it)" (xiii). Neel suggests that in order for strong public discourse to exist,

> the writer and the speaker must escape the binary opposition between idealism and deconstruction and begin to write—an

act that encompasses and exceeds both Plato and Derrida. Protagoras and Gorgias reveal the way by anticipating deconstruction, undermining Platonism, and using rhetoric to show how one recognizes a good decision and helps it prevail. (xiii)

Neel describes three kinds of writing that result from his reading of the *Phaedrus*. "Soul writing" is the surface representation of an internal dialectical pursuit of possible truth, yet once inscribed and thus no longer representing this dialectical process, it ceases to exist as soul writing. "Psophistry" (the silent *p* distinguishes Plato's sophistry from that of the other sophists) is writing that represses the dialectical process in pursuit of possible truth, inscribing instead the appearance of certainty, a single position presented as right and true. Finally, "anti-writing" is the vacuous, prestructured prose of the five-paragraph theme, which, according to Neel, sounds like this:

> I am not writing. I hold no position. I have nothing at all to do with discovery, communication, or persuasion. I care nothing about the truth. What I *am* is an essay. I announce my beginning, my parts, my ending, and the links between them. I announce myself as sentences correctly punctuated and words correctly spelled. (85)

Psophistry (the repression of valid opposition) and anti-writing (the refusal to acknowledge any position at all) are the dominant modes of writing in modern composition classes.

Neel's reading of Derrida's early works on deconstruction reveals two kinds of writing: "writing in the *narrow* sense" and "writing in the *general* sense." First, in narrow writing (or classical writing), inscription attempts to re-present speech, which re-presents thought. Yet with each remove (from thought to speech to writing), impurities are introduced (such as différance, repetition, replacement, and absence), since speech can never be a perfect replica of thought, and writing can never be a perfect replica of speech. Most Western writing and certainly most of the writing done in American composition classes attempt to mask the play of différance, repetition, replacement, and absence in the writing process, making writing appear *as pure as thought itself,* and if writing is unable to mask its own instability, then it is devalued as impure. According to Neel:

Because everything Western that would count as thinking appears in writing, the devaluation of writing plays a crucial role. First, it allows the formation and integrity of the individual as an absolute origin of meaning; second, it keeps meaning intact by constantly calling attention to itself as an inadequate servant to the greater truth it attempts to bear. . . . By conceiving writing as the replacement for speech, by treating it as an inadequate medium for capturing the meaning that simply emerges in speech, the illusion of pure meaning lives on. (118–19)

However, "Throughout an enormous and painstaking set of readings," Neel points out, "Derrida has tried to show that all the characteristics of writing in the narrow sense—all the deficiencies that make it tertiary, repetitive, metaphoric, and metonymic—also exist in speaking, also exist in thinking, exist even in Being" (112). In fact, "when one tries to work back to the level that precedes, founds, and enables writing [that is, to thought itself], one finds nothing more than the exact same operation of writing—supplement, repetition, différance, absence" (113). According to Derrida, then, writing is not an imperfect representation of pure thought but rather thought resembles and is enabled by the processes and structures of signification that are characteristic of writing. General writing, then, is writing that acknowledges this play of differences, the inevitable absence of that which is sought, and it gives no pretense of representing pure thought and meaning.

Neel concludes *Plato, Derrida, and Writing* with a plea for what he calls strong discourse, a kind of writing that is inherently *rhetorical,* not philosophical. According to Neel:

What exempts rhetoric and writing from any condemnation by philosophy is that all philosophy, including Platonism and deconstruction, is both written and rhetorical. Rhetoric, as the sophists tried to explain so many years ago, is the prior medium in which the possibility and impossibility of truth play out an endless struggle. (203)

Neel argues that private or philosophical discourse (including Plato's soul writing and Derrida's general writing) is "weak because it remains untested in the arena of public life" (208). However, it is crucial that we not

> underestimate the attraction of weak discourse, for it always
> presents itself in the guise of the messiah or philosopher-
> king—the one who claims to offer truth but in fact supplies
> only the silence that must occur when rhetoric, persuasion,
> writing, and sophistry, those most human of things, have been
> precluded. (209)

Yet, in contrast, Neel suggests, "Any discourse that has been expressed
publicly and found adherents becomes strong, deriving its strength from
its ability to withstand the scrutiny of public life" (208). Strong discourse
is inherently sophistic, relying on relativistic epistemologies and the belief
in the persuasive power of *logos,* and these views of knowledge and language are derived, according to Neel, from the doctrines of Gorgias and
Protagoras (204–8). The ultimate strength of sophistic strong discourse

> lies first in the sophists' awareness of how rhetoric and writ-
> ing create belief and action; second in the sophists' willing-
> ness to hold all belief permanently in question (without dis-
> believing); and third in the sophists' ability to take action only
> when that action can support itself with a strong discourse,
> a discourse whose history of general persuasiveness is long
> and whose opposite has been given every opportunity to be
> heard. (208)

And it is this sophistic strong discourse that must become the preoccu-
pation of composition teachers and students if we are to prepare new
generations to participate in the flow of public life.

Ten years after Crowley published "Of Gorgias and Grammatology," she turned her neosophistic musings away from poststructuralism proper and more toward what might loosely be called pragmatism, a theoretical shift that would be developed in later years by Steven
Mailloux. In "A Plea for the Revival of Sophistry," Crowley offers the
rhetorical theory and practice of the older sophists as an antidote to the
stifling "technologized rhetorics" that foreground universal rules at the
expense of situational adaptation. According to Crowley, "Because of
their practical focus, the Sophists were able to face squarely the fact that
not one but several interpretations of any given state of affairs are often in competition with one another, and that choices must be made
among them" (328). The problem for modern composition studies,
however, is that most writing teachers do not view themselves or their
students as participants in any larger social formation. From the older

sophists, then, composition teachers learn that "those who are engaged in teaching discursive practice . . . cannot escape the public aspect of their work," and thus they are "always engaged in Sophistry" (330). Rhetoric is a pragmatic art; its success lies not in its universal technologies but in its adaptability to infinitely varied contexts.

Several of the essays in Mailloux's edited collection *Rhetoric, Sophistry, Pragmatism* extend Crowley's earlier claims, elaborating the more specific argument that "neopragmatism can be viewed as a postmodernist form of sophistic rhetoric" (2). In his introduction, "Sophistry and Rhetorical Pragmatism," Mailloux demonstrates that the founders of the pragmatist movement at the turn of the century were keenly aware that sophistic doctrines were, in many ways, important precursors to pragmatist epistemologies. In particular, early pragmatists (such as William James, John Dewey, and F. C. S. Schiller) and more recent neopragmatists (such as Richard Rorty and Stanley Fish) acknowledge Protagoras's "man-measure" doctrine as the ancient foundation for twentieth-century pragmatist epistemologies. Throughout the twentieth century, relativistic pragmatist epistemologies have been criticized for their focus on practical wisdom and their denial of absolute truth, and this reference to Protagorean relativism lends a certain anti-Platonic credibility to the arguments advanced by contemporary (neo)pragmatists.

Other essays in Mailloux's collection advance different connections between the ancient sophists and contemporary pragmatism. According to Edward Schiappa,

> Three interrelated themes in Isocrates's writings that have obvious contemporary pragmatism parallels are his regard for the importance of informed opinion *(doxa)* and doubts about certainty *(epistêmê)*; his belief that pedagogy ought to be moral and aimed at preparing students for participation in civic affairs; and his general preference for practical over speculative philosophy. (57)

Don H. Bialostosky is somewhat more purposeful in his appropriation of sophistic (dialogic) rhetoric, directly opposing it to monologic institutionalized discourses. According to Bialostosky, "sophistic rhetoric joins Bakhtin's dialogics in treating official discourse as one kind of discourse, however locally and temporally powerful, that must hold its own over time against other discourses that criticize its decisions and challenge its authority" (91). Bialostosky considers the neopragmatic recovery of sophistic and Bakhtinian rhetoric to be a kind of "homecoming" that is both celebratory and contestatory in nature. It is

> an occasion on which those who have long since left an in-
> stitution and been forgotten by it are invited back and ral-
> lied by those now in possession of it to support their struggle
> with an opposing institution. For such purposes, the soph-
> ists, the verbal-liberal arts, and Bakhtin himself are welcome
> back. (93)

Whether viewed in relation to poststructuralist relativism or pragmatist public discourse, sophistic rhetoric contributes antidotes to stifling foundational epistemologies and the universal rules of technologized rhetoric. While the political projects of poststructuralists like
Crowley and Neel and neopragmatists like Mailloux and Bialostosky are
fairly general in their scope, other neosophists choose more specific
projects, developing approaches that have come to be known as feminist sophistics and third sophistics.

Feminist and Third Sophistics

In "The Feminist Sophistic Enterprise," Audrey Wick argues that there
are striking similarities between the historical situations that gave rise
to sophistry in the fifth century BCE and the historical situations that gave
rise to feminism in the 1960s and 1970s, with the pressures of war
(Peloponnesian and Vietnam) and political revolution (new democratic
governance and the civil rights movement) most prominent among them.
But Wick's most pressing interest in sophistic rhetoric is its exploration
of the *nomos* (truth as social construct) versus *phusis* (truth inscribed
in nature) opposition, and she applies this opposition to feminist studies as well. "Like the sophists," Wick says, "some feminists are intensely
interested in exploring *phusis* and *nomos*. One school of feminists argues that men and women have essentially different natures and that
these natures are reflected in . . . matriarchal myths." Another school,
however, seeks to "excavate the origins of our myths hoping to show
that all differences are cultural and not biological, and hence changeable" (30). For Wick, then, many of the problematics that the sophists
were forced to confront over twenty-five centuries ago are the same
problematics faced by feminists today.

Susan Jarratt approaches the older sophists (as well as her own version of neosophistry) through feminist theory and critical pedagogy. In

Rereading the Sophists, Jarratt argues that foundational metaphysics are inherently oppressive: they encourage hierarchical classifications according to race, class, and gender, always favoring one classification over any other (63–65). Jarratt finds an alternative to the oppressive logic of foundational metaphysics in the sophistic concept *nomos* (which she defines as social customs or conventional behavior). *Nomos,* according to Jarratt, "offers a mode of reading centered on narratives encoded in the text and in the times. Such an analytic provides a useful alternative to the attempt to discover marginalized voices marked by characteristic stylistic features" (75).

In particular, feminist (neo)sophistics employs *nomos* and narrative to undermine the "falsely naturalized logic of patriarchy" (76) and to reread texts (literary and historical) so that voices formerly silenced by foundational metaphysics may be heard and understood. Jarratt concludes her discussion of the first sophists and feminism with the following reflection:

> What I have discovered through this exploration is that, though the sophists may not be "feminists," current feminists are becoming sophists in the best sense of the word by describing rhetorical solutions to the crucial problems of defining a theory with the most power for changing women's lives. Sophistic rhetoric enables a feminist reading/writing practice of breaking into the "received histories" of the discourse of man. Rewriting/rereading texts in terms of the narrative logic of difference opens avenues not only in literature but also in the history of rhetoric. Narratizing the social-historical differential specifically in rhetoric will trace the diversion of women's discursive energy into the school room and drawing room, allowing a redefined "rhetoric" to include letters, texts on manners and education, and perhaps other forms as yet unidentified. It allows not only for the identification of new works but also offers a way to reread hegemonic texts as well, tracing the itinerary of male desire with a new critical perspective. Showing how feminist theory and literary critical work enact practices adumbrated by the democratic rhetoric of the sophists provides a way to recover a range of marginal voices in the history of rhetoric. Reciprocally, outlining the connections with sophistic rhetoric in current feminist reading and writing may offer increased leverage for dis-

lodging the patriarchal institutions whose foundations were
laid during the sophists' time. (78–79)

Jarratt's move from logic to narrative and from *phusis* to *nomos* con-
firms her neosophistic and feminist approaches to rhetorical theory as
epistemic, and her neosophistic epistemic rhetoric fights against the socially exclusionary nature of language in order to give voice to the otherwise muted and marginalized.

In the final chapter of *Rereading the Sophists,* Jarratt turns her critical attention toward writing pedagogy, and she draws on sophistic teaching methods as a means to solve current problems in composition studies. Here Jarratt's goal is "to examine the sophists' educational praxis
within the direct democracy of Athens as a way of reflecting on the political possibilities for composition teaching today" (81), and, she continues, "analyzing the relationships among the first sophists' social
theory, their pedagogy, and the functioning of the democracy in their time
can help us evaluate the political dimensions of composition pedagogies
in our own" (82). Jarratt limits her commentary to one school of thought
in particular, critical pedagogy, whose practitioners—such as Paulo Freire,
Stanley Aronowitz, Henry Giroux, and Ira Shor—"revive the goals of
the first sophists" (107). According to Jarratt, both the ancient sophists
and modern critical pedagogues teach (and taught) critical consciousness or the systematic demystification of institutionalized discourses.
Both the sophists and critical pedagogues demystify (and demystified)
these oppressive discourses by exposing their inherent contradictions—
the sophists by means of exploring the *dissoi logoi* (two-fold or opposing arguments) in any given situation and the critical pedagogues by
deconstructing dominant discourses. For these politically committed
ancients and moderns, demystification inevitably leads to emancipation.

Both Wick's and Jarratt's notions of feminist sophistics and sophistic critical pedagogy involve a negative dialectical methodology, one in
which the oppositions of dominant discourse are simply reversed rather
than destroyed. According to Victor Vitanza, however, this "negative"
form of deconstruction does little to abolish dominant discourses, merely
re-inscribing new dominant discourses in place of the old ones. Instead,
Vitanza suggests, we should not favor men over women or women over
men; we should deconstruct the very act of favoring itself. Based on
deconstructive methodologies described by Gayatri Spivak and Derrida,
Vitanza argues that any negative deconstruction (the point at which
Jarratt stops) must be followed by *affirmative* deconstruction. Vitanza

continues, "while the first [negative deconstruction] stays in the binary, the second [affirmative deconstruction] calls out to the other so as perhaps to pass out of the binary to countless genders and sexes" (*Negation* 219). And passing out of binary thought, calling out to the "excluded third" (as opposed to elevating the marginalized "other") is the postmodern basis for Vitanza's "Third Sophistic."

For Vitanza, the subject/object relation that inevitably exists in any binary opposition, whether man/woman or woman/man, is politically problematic. Instead, rhetoric and its practitioners should reach out to the third other, beyond subject/object relations, destroying in the process the very foundations on which binary logic rests. In "'Some More' Notes, Toward a 'Third' Sophistic," Vitanza describes this postmodern sophistic critical attitude in some detail:

> A *Third Sophistic,* or *Postmodern/ParaRhetoric,* would be, or *is,* an "art" of "resisting and disrupting" the available means (that is, the cultural codes) that allow for persuasion and identification; the "art" of not only refusing the available (capitalistic/socialist) codes but also of refusing altogether to recode, or to reterritorialize, power relations whether they be manifested in the ideologies of a State Philosophy, Ethic, or Religion. . . . A *Third Sophistic Rhetoric* is interested in perpetual decodification and deterritorialization. Moreover, it has *no* faith whatsoever in the "game of knowledge" or the "grand narrative of emancipation." It sees both as tragic traps in which human beings wish to find/found themselves, to give themselves to conscious-suppression, unconscious-repression, and political-oppression. (133).

It is only this *Third* Sophistic that can lead, in the final analysis, to true equality—not through struggle and emancipation but through the affirmative deconstruction of oppressive foundations.

It is anachronistic and generally unhelpful to argue that Gorgias articulated an ancient theory of epistemic, pragmatic, feminist, or postmodern rhetoric; it is quite useful, however, to explore the ways in which certain elements of Gorgianic rhetoric can solve (and have solved) problems in the articulation of contemporary theories of rhetoric. I would like to reassert here that the categories of neosophistic rhetoric presented above are not mutually exclusive; they are intended only to guide inquiry, not to essentialize the different neosophists as one thing or another. Indeed, all of the neosophists discussed above are united in their *appropriative* use of sophistic doctrines. Each turns, though in different ways and for different reasons, to the rhetoric of fifth-century BCE Greece for inspiration, for solutions to contemporary problems whether in rhetorical, pedagogical, or administrative arenas. It is probably fair to say that epistemic rhetoric, rhetorical pragmatism, and certainly feminist and third sophistics would not exist, as they do now, without the profound influence of the sophists in Athens.

4
Postmodern Sophistics

In chapter 3, I examine a variety of neosophists who explicitly appropriate ancient sophistic doctrines for the purpose of solving problems in contemporary rhetoric and composition studies. In this fourth chapter, however, my focus turns away from self-conscious appropriation to what I call postmodern sophistics. I argue that contemporary postmodern critical theory is sophistic in terms of its epistemic foundations and characteristic rhetorical strategies. Particularly in the works of Kenneth Burke, Jean-François Lyotard, Jean Baudrillard, and Jacques Derrida, certain postmodern concepts bear remarkable resemblances to fifth-century BCE Gorgianic concepts. In this chapter, first, I will explore postmodern sophistic theories of representation and, second, apply these theories of representation to an emerging form of discourse that I call postmodern epideictic rhetoric or graffitic immemorial discourse.

One of the central problematics among sophists, whether ancient or postmodern, concerns the nature of *representation* or the relationship between language and what it represents. The most naïve understanding of representation views language as transparent, a pure medium through which reality may be described and understood without distortion. But a more sophistic(ated) understanding of representation views language as a highly problematic medium, one that transforms its referent irretrievably into something else.

Sophistic Representation

In all three of his major texts, Gorgias treats in very direct ways the problem of representation, but his discussion of representation is nowhere more clear than in the third section of *On Non-Existence*. Here Gorgias argues for the radical disconnection of language from reality:

> For *logos* is the means by which we communicate, but *logos* is different from substances and existent things. Thus we do not communicate existent things to our neighbors; instead we communicate only *logos,* which is something other than substances. Certainly, just as the visible would not become audible and vice versa, so external existence (as substances) would not become our *logos;* and as something other than *logos,* external existence could not be revealed to another person. And indeed Gorgias says that *logos* is produced when realities (that is, perceivable objects) strike us from outside. For when we experience a flavor, we generate *logos* regarding that quality; and when we see a color, we generate *logos* regarding that color. But if this is so, then *logos* is not a representation of the external, but the external becomes the signifier of *logos*. (B3.84–85)

In presophistic myth and natural philosophy, language was assumed to correspond accurately to that which it re-presented; thus, the cultural content of myths and the universal content of the natural world were the most fruitful intellectual pursuits, not language, since language was only viewed as the transparent mirror of myth and nature. But Gorgias, in *On Non-Existence,* separates *logos* (broadly conceived as language) from *pragmata* (the things to which language refers) in an effort to validate the study of language.

Commenting on the same passage quoted above from *On Non-Existence,* Walker Gibson notes:

> These sentiments will sound familiar to many a late-twentieth-century mind. The uneasy relation of symbol to thing symbolized is an issue now commonplace in almost every discipline, and it should be sobering to recognize that it was an issue for Sophists twenty-four centuries ago. (285)

While the political reasons for this separation of symbol and thing were different in ancient times from our political reasons today, there is, nevertheless, a similar attempt in postmodern critical theory to separate the medium from the object of representation.

Postmodern Sophistic Representation

In "Periodizing the '60s," Fredric Jameson notes that the "critique of representation" is an important element of "postmodernism generally" (194). For most postmodern critical theorists, the process through which language derives meaning and the political consequences of this process are more complicated than the simplistic ways Enlightenment semiotic theories represent them. But if art does not re-present reality, if language does not re-present truth and reason, if a signifier does not re-present a signified—if there is no "re-presentation" (as Western metaphysics has understood the concept since Plato)—what is the cost to rhetoric?

Enlightenment theories of art, language, and criticism assume an accurate correspondence between signifier and signified, between re-presentation and reality: the painting, short story, essay (to take it a step further, any utterance, or any meaningful "action" as opposed to "motion," in Burke's terminology) is merely the surface feature manifestation of some deeper, more vital truth, reason, or structure—and to reveal this truth/reason/structure is the *telos* (end or goal) of interpretation. A postmodern semiotics, however, rejects this content/form correspondence in favor of a form/form dialectic. In relativistic postmodern theory, then, the formal properties of a signifier do not re-present some reality or deep structure meaning transported unchanged from the signified; rather, these formal properties refer to the formal properties of other representations. There is no originary event, experience, reality, or truth on which verbal and visual texts are based; every event and experience is an intertextual conglomeration of semiotic significance. All texts, then, refer to (but do not re-present) other texts; they actively appropriate meaning (selectively, politically) from past texts (through direct reference, for example) as much as past texts appropriate the space of new texts (through trace and dissemination) as continuations and transferences of their own political purposes. This notion of intertextuality implies a dialectical construction of meaning: past texts infuse new texts with cultural significance, both rejuvenating meaning in past texts and conditioning meaning in new texts; and new texts appropriate cultural significance from past texts, both reconditioning the historical significance of past texts and legitimating the political efforts of new texts.

This turn from the modernist content/form correspondence to the postmodern form/form dialectic has definite consequences: when signifieds are removed from the equation of semiotic meaning, then "reality" becomes metareality, reconstructed in each new context and in each new encounter with human perception; reality, in other words, is always already a politicized representation with no originary presence, and discourse is always already metadiscourse. The formal properties of signifiers, then, play off the formal properties of other signifiers, never hoping for originary Truth but always hoping to seduce audiences into new contexts, contexts in which "meaning" is unstable and politically charged. It is through the language we use and the contexts in which we use it that meaning is constructed; and our constructions of meaning and reality are always purposeful, always political, and always bear the markers of the institutional power structures that give rise to and condition representational constructions of reality and meaning. Burke, Lyotard, Baudrillard, and Derrida have influenced this conception of postmodern politicized representation in a number of ways, and it is with their theories of language and meaning that I will be concerned for the next few pages. Because each has politically represented postmodern representation in unique ways, I will consider each theorist's work in turn.

Most scholars in the Humanities recognize 1966 as the year that poststructuralism made its way from the European continent to America: this is the landmark year that Derrida presented "Structure, Sign, and Play in the Discourse of the Human Sciences" at a conference titled "The Languages of Criticism and the Sciences of Man" held at Johns Hopkins University (Lodge 107). While Derrida's "Structure, Sign, and Play" indeed constitutes a landmark moment in the history of critical theory, it is important to note that Burke had articulated a similar critique of structuralist re-presentation some years prior to the Johns Hopkins conference. Though not completely poststructuralist or postmodern in his thinking about language and meaning, Burke does put aside his Enlightenment ideals in his discussions of entitlement and terministic screens.

In "What Are the Signs of What? (A Theory of 'Entitlement')," originally published in 1962, Burke inverts the "commonsense" (or structuralist) idea that "words are the signs of things" and instead explores the proposition that "things are the signs of words" (360–61). Burke asks:

> Might words be found to possess a "spirit" particular to their nature as words? And might the things of experience then become in effect the materialization of such spirit, the manifestation of this spirit in visible tangible bodies? . . . If such verbal spirits, or essences, were enigmatically symbolized in nonverbal things, then their derivation (so far as causes with-

in the natural world are concerned) could come both from the forms of language and from the group motives that language possesses by reason of its nature as a social product. (361)

Burke argues that we should think of language as "the 'entitling' of complex nonverbal situations"; that is,

> in mediating between the social realm and the realm of nonverbal nature, words communicate to things the spirit that the society imposes upon the words which have come to be the "names" for them. The things are in effect the visible tangible material embodiments of the spirit that infuses them through the medium of words. (361–62)

Language, then, does not re-present things and ideas; instead, it infuses things and ideas with socially constructed meaning, with meaning derived from the interaction of linguistic and rhetorical forces within a cultural context. Particular social groups, or "tribes" as Burke would say, develop (through myths, religions, and customs) a common language that allows individual members to understand the nonverbal world in characteristically similar ways, through what Burke later called "terministic screens."

In "Terministic Screens" (one of the five summarizing essays in *Language as Symbolic Action* and originally published in 1965), Burke sets up his dramatistic approach to language in opposition to the more common scientistic (or structuralist) approach to language. According to Burke, in the scientistic approach, "the power of language to define and describe may be viewed as derivative" (44). Language, in other words, derives its power directly from the power of the reality it re-presents. However, a dramatistic approach to the power of language reverses the equation. Burke argues that "various tribal idioms are unquestionably *developed* by their use as instruments in the tribe's way of living" (44); language is created and maintained in its pragmatic cultural uses, and through symbolic action it constructs the realities that constitute the material conditions of a social group or tribe. Although Burke does not reject all forms of reference, he does, like Derrida and other poststructuralists, locate meaning in language rather than in reality itself. Burke argues, for example, "Even if any given terminology is a *reflection* of reality, by its very nature as a terminology it must be a *selection* of reality; and to this extent it must function also as a *deflection* of reality" (45). So even if we grant language its referential function, which Burke is willing to do only to a degree, we must still acknowledge that it is only through language that we can understand reality. And since language is developed through its use in cultural contexts, Burke concludes, we must assume that certain cultural nomenclatures of terminology condition our perceptions. These nomenclatures, or terministic screens, make the way one talks about an object or event a political act, an instance of symbolic action.

While Burke's theories of entitlement and terministic screens may have had little direct impact on continental postmodern philosophies of representation, there are, nevertheless, striking similarities. Lyotard enters the modern/postmodern debate over representation through Sigmund Freud's theories of psychoanalytic interpretation. For Lyotard, Freud's applied psychoanalysis neglects the choices (unconscious or deliberate) that artists make in creating their works. Freud assumes that the deep meaning of a work determines its formal properties, thus treating the art object "as a surface to be penetrated." Artistic representations, therefore, (in Freud's interpretive scheme) serve only a "substitutive or vicarious function." An art object exists in the place of some other object that is missing, "and they are there only *because* the [other] object is missing." Lyotard's postmodern aesthetic, on the other hand, calls attention to the "affirmative character of works" ("Beyond" 158). In "Beyond Representation," Lyotard explains the ontological status of art objects from a postmodern perspective:

> They are not in place of anything; they do not *stand for* but stand; that is to say, they function through their material and its organization (not an inevitable or necessary organization); and it conceals no content, no libidinal secret of the work, whose force lies entirely in its surface. There is only surface. (158)

Here Lyotard rejects the Freudian (and modernist) notion of deep-structure meaning in favor of a form/form dialectic, a semiotics of surface play. This notion of surface play is necessitated by Lyotard's rejection of the traditional rhetorical triangle in *The Differend*. Lyotard argues there that the addressor (encoder), addressee (decoder), and referent (past text/s) are vital elements in every communicative situation, but it is mainly in his notion of sense that Lyotard differs from modernist theorists (13). Communication proceeds because the existence of the referent is assumed, but communication is problematized when the interlocutors presuppose different senses (or representations, governed by personal experiences and social predispositions) of the referent. The modernist model of communication, lacking this notion of sense, assumes that disputes may be settled simply by referring to the referent in question (whether through empirical observation or logical deduction). However, as Lyotard suggests, a postmodern model of communication assumes that any transcendentalism or universality of the referent is thwarted by the differing senses or representations of the referent that interlocutors presuppose. Economic, political, and social forces in our personal and cultural histories construct our epistemologies, which in turn construct the senses we derive from various referents.

Lyotard discusses the consequences of the modernist conception of representation in *Heidegger and "the jews."* There Lyotard suggests that the true function of modernist representation is not to re-present (or even illuminate) a given reality but rather to conceal competing politicized representations, to make us admire the (supposed) re-presentation and forget other representations (3–5). In this respect, modernist re-presentation serves a sociopolitical function: those in possession of the powers of language and mass media also hold power over representation, power over what is remembered and what is forgotten—power over knowledge itself. As Lyotard suggests, the postmodern desire to break free from this re-presentation-induced trance "means to fight against forgetting the precariousness of what has been established, of the reestablished past" (10). Art and language, therefore, do not re-present reality; they establish new realities that replace those they represent. Lyotard's surface play becomes a vital postmodern alternative to the modernist illusion of re-presentation: language refers to language both as trace and as context but does not re-present reality; and art refers to art as trace and context but does not re-present any deep-structure meaning. Language and art play a game of surface semiotics, and the rules of this game require active participation in the play of representations, in the construction of experience, and in the agon of ideas. It is only through generating counter-representations that social change can occur.

Baudrillard, like Lyotard, enters the debate over representation through Freud's works, most clearly articulating in *Seduction* his discontentment with theories of psychoanalytic interpretation. Psychoanalytic interpretation assumes that latent discourse turns manifest discourse toward truth and meaning. Thus, this manifest discourse "has the status of an appearance, a laboured appearance, transversed by the emergence of meaning." And in Freudian psychoanalysis, interpretation "breaks the appearance and play of the manifest discourse and, by taking up with the latent discourse, delivers the real meaning" (53). But Baudrillard rejects psychoanalytic interpretation as a valuable terministic screen through which to understand the world. Instead, Baudrillard offers seduction as a postmodern practice for our postmodern culture. Seduction, in contrast to interpretation, turns the manifest discourse back on the latent discourse "in order to invalidate it, substituting the charm and illusion of appearances" (53). Deep structure meaning, in the Freudian sense, does not exist—only illusion and appearance (simulacra) exist. Originary reference (that is, reference to reality, Truth) is replaced with reference to models that have no identifiable origin. Seduction, according to Baudrillard, "represents mastery over the symbolic universe" (8); the "only thing truly at stake is mastery of the strategy of appearances, against the force of being and reality" (10).

Throughout much of his work, Baudrillard (again, like Lyotard) also develops a theory of representation as surface play. Language and art assume the form of simulations and simulacra in Baudrillard's postmodern world. In *Simulations,* Baudrillard argues that while modernist representers try to make their linguistic representations coincide with the real, "simulators," on the other hand, "try to make the real, all the real, coincide with their simulation models" (2). The real, in the modernist sense, vanishes entirely, and "[w]ith it goes all of metaphysics" (3). "Simulation," for Baudrillard, "begins with the liquidation of all referentials" (4). It is only when the signified is erased that the signifier may be considered a social construction and representation may be considered politicized. Baudrillard describes four "successive phases of the image" in recent history: first, the image is "the reflection of a basic reality"; second, it "masks and perverts a basic reality"; third, it "masks the *absence* of a basic reality"; and fourth, "it bears no relation to any reality whatever: it is its own pure simulacrum" (11). In the first two phases of the image, a basic reality is presupposed, and the image reflects or masks that reality. In the third and fourth phases, however, reality itself is an image. These final two stages mark the age of the precession of models, of simulacra, in which images constitute our realities, images so real-seeming that they are "more real than the real." This is the age of simulation, which Baudrillard defines as "the generation by models of a real without origin or reality: a hyperreal" (2). In the third and fourth stages of the image, the "representational imaginary . . . disappears with simulation." And with the loss of this representational imaginary "goes all of metaphysics. No more mirror of being and its appearances, of the real and its concept." Here the "real is produced from miniaturized units, from matrices, memory banks, and command models—and with these it can be reproduced an indefinite number of times" (3). Re-presentation "starts from the principle that the sign and the real are equivalent." Simulation starts, conversely, "*from the radical negation of the sign as value*, from the sign as reversion and death sentence of every reference" (11).

While Lyotard and Baudrillard approach the problem of representation through Freudian psychoanalysis, Derrida approaches the issue of representation through his conception of translation and through his notions of play, trace, différance, and dissemination. Derrida, along with many of his postmodern colleagues, rejects the notion that language and art re-present some absolute Truth, universal meaning, or transcendental signified. The key to understanding Derrida's approach to representation is to see that he speaks of two completely different conceptions of representation, one modernist/structuralist and unacceptable (which he critiques) and the other postmodernist/poststructuralist and necessary (which he accepts). Derrida rejects the modernist closure of re-presentation but leaves room (as Lyotard and Baudrillard do) for a postmodern representation of play, trace, différance, and dissemination.

For Derrida, representation is necessary for communication to succeed; however, it is the closure of modernist re-presentation to which Derrida objects. Modernist re-presentation achieves closure through two faulty assumptions: (1) that the thing represented is a universal presence that transcends contextual influences on meaning and (2) that representation *re*-presents this presence in a different but perfectly parallel semiotic code (see "Sending" 295–326, *Speech* 48–59, and "Theater" 232–43). Derrida elaborates his conception of modernist representation in "Sending" through the example of translation. The modernist view of translation presupposes "an invariable identity of sense" behind every word or semantic unit, and every language would re-present that invariable sense in the same way (303). So with a universal referent, a transcendental signified as its foundation, different languages may be freely substituted, one for another, without loss or distortion of meaning and sense. According to Derrida:

> This hypothesis or this desire would be precisely that of representation, of a representative language whose object would be to represent something (to represent in all the senses of the delegation of presence, of reiteration rendering present once again, in substituting a presentation for another *in absentia* and so on); such a language would represent something, a sense,

an object, a referent, indeed even another representation in whatever sense, which would be anterior and exterior to it. Under the diversity of words from diverse languages, under the diversity of the uses of the same word, under the diversity of contexts or of syntactic systems, the same sense or the same referent, the same representative content would keep its inviolable identity. Language, every language would be representative, a system of representatives, but the content represented, what is represented by this representation (a meaning, a thing, and so on) would be a presence and not a representation. What is represented would not have the structure of representation, the representative structure of the representative. Language would be a system of representatives or also of signifiers, of place-holders *(lieu-tenants)* substituted for what they say, signify, or represent, and the equivocal diversity of the representatives would not affect the unity, the identity, indeed even the ultimate simplicity of the represented. ("Sending" 303–4)

Modernist re-presentation, embodied within this traditional conception of the nature of translation, assumes that language, in its re-presentational function, substitutes a present reality with an identical copy. And since different languages copy present realities in identical ways, it is easy to jump from copy to copy and never lose track of the reality that each copy re-presents. However, as we will see, Derrida rejects this modernist conception of re-presentation as substitution.

Like Lyotard and Baudrillard, Derrida counters the modernist belief in the universality of signification through a semiotics of context. Modernist philosophy, according to Derrida, "pushes the word to its very greatest obscurity, in a highly artificial way, in abstracting it from every context and every use value, as if a word were to regulate itself on a concept independently of any contextualized function" ("Sending" 301). This practice is, of course, misleading, since all language exists within a specific context that saturates communication with politicized meaning. Derrida elaborates:

If I read, if I hear on the radio that the diplomatic or parliamentary representatives of some country have been received by the Chief of State, that representatives of striking workers or the parents of schoolchildren have gone to the Ministry in a delegation, if I read in the paper that this evening there will be a representation of some play, or that such and such a painting represents this or that, etc., I understand without the least equivocation and I do not put my head into my hands to take in what it means. It is clearly enough for me to have the competence required in a certain state of society and of its educational system. . . . Given that words always function in an (assumed) context destined to assure in the normal way the normality of their functioning, to ask what they can mean before and outside every such determined context is to study (it might perhaps be said) a pathology or a linguistic dysfunction. The schema is well known. Philosophical questioning about the name and the essence of "representation" before and outside of every particular context would be the very paradigm of this dysfunction. It would necessarily lead to insoluble problems or to pointless language games, or rather to language games which the philosopher would take seriously without perceiving what, in the functioning of language, makes the game possible. In this perspective it would not be a question of excluding philosophical styles or models from ordinary language but of acknowledging their place among others. What we have made of the word "representation" as philosophers in the last centuries or decades would come to be integrated, more or less well, into the ensemble of codes and usages. This also would be a contextual possibility among others. ("Sending" 319–20)

In the modernist search for universal meaning, this pathology or dysfunction, as Derrida calls it, is always foiled by a reference to context. There can be no transcendental signified when context (rather than some universal semantic kernel) determines meaning.

If context saturates language with meaning and if there is no transcendental signified to which one may refer to regularize and universalize communication and, finally, if representation is *not* to be thrown out entirely, what shape must representation take in order to function in this semiotics of situation? Derrida solves the problem by revealing that modernist re-presentation is not re-presentation at all. Since the re-presentation assumes a different context than the original presentation it substitutes, it must also, then, assume a different meaning, independent of any shared semantic kernel. The only truly repetitive, reproductive re-presentation is, Derrida argues, one based on dissemination, not present-being. In dissemination, trace and différance forever and unavoidably re-present themselves throughout all communication. Trace and différance appear in communication in the form of *renvois,* a sending back ("Sending" 324). The problem of the modernist closure of representation is solved, for Derrida, in this deferral to the socially constructed and politicized representation of trace and différance in each new context. For Derrida, then, the modernist conception of presence is fallacious, since all "presence" is by virtue of trace and différance politicized representation.

These postmodern representations of representation (by Burke, Lyotard, Baudrillard, and Derrida) intersect in interesting ways with Gorgias's sophistic representation of representation. First, for Gorgias and Burke, language does not re-present reality; rather, reality is the representation of language, since language is the force that gives meaning and intelligibility to the things that surround us. In the third thesis of *On Non-Existence,* Gorgias writes, "*logos* is not a representation of the external, but the external becomes the signifier of *logos*" (B3.85). This is a remarkable passage that anticipates Burke's "What Are the Signs of What?" and Leff's "In Search of Ariadne's Thread" by more than twenty-four hundred years. If language infuses existence with meaning and order, then existence is the surface manifestation of human language and thought; and when cultures influence the acquisition and use of language, then reality itself must be viewed as socially constructed, as *rhetorical.*

Second, for Gorgias, Lyotard, and Baudrillard, if reality has any impact on language, it is uncertain at best, since meaning undergoes a sort of transformation in the interpretive processes of perception. What we convey, in other words, is *logos,* not reality, and the *logos* we convey becomes an altogether different *logos* once it is received by an interlocutor. And even if reality did not undergo such a transformation in the perceptual processes, the imperfect nature of human understanding inhibits access to any kind of "true" knowledge. Gorgias suggests in the *Encomium of Helen* that if humans had accurate memories of the past, true conceptions of the present, and reliable foresight of the future, then language would not have an unstable effect on audiences. However, since it is difficult for audiences to remember the past, scrutinize the present, and foresee the future, language cannot function by reference to some deep-structure meaning, for no such meaning exists. Instead, much of language's effect comes from the formal properties of structure and style (recall, however, that in public debate and poetry, these effects can often be negative).

Finally, for Gorgias and Derrida, the context of communication has as much to do with meaning as the matter that is communicated. Gorgias and Derrida, in other words, both argue that language is the result of situational constraints and conditions that, as Gorgias describes, "strike us from outside" (*On Non-Existence* B3.84). Thus, if rhetoric does not consider the context of communication, it misses fully half of the meaning that is generated in any given situation. In the *Defense of Palamedes,* Gorgias highlights the importance of rhetorical context in the title character's discussion of ethos. In order to defend himself against Odysseus's charge of treason, Palamedes must prove that his own ethos is above such reproach. In ancient Greece, however, self-praise was considered a violation of social decorum—*except* in a court case where one's character was being questioned. Thus, in this particular rhetorical situation (as opposed to many other possible situations), although Palamedes engages in self-praise, it is appropriate because the *context* allows and even necessitates it.

Although Gorgias and the postmodern sophists are separated by nearly twenty-five hundred years, and the contexts that gave rise to their writings are indeed different, their descriptions of how language derives meaning are remarkably similar. In the next section of this chapter, I explore the rhetorical consequences of this postmodern/sophistic view of representation in specific relation to epideictic rhetoric. What I call postmodern epideictic rhetoric or graffitic immemorial discourse is a postmodern/sophistic rhetorical strategy based on the assumption that any use of language is necessarily political and context bound.

Postmodern Epideictic Rhetoric: Graffitic Immemorial Discourse

Rhetorical genres are historical constructs generated from the exigencies of particular economic, political, and sociocultural situations; and as these situations shift, so, too, must our conceptions of the characteristic forms and functions of rhetorical genres. In *Learning to Curse,* Stephen J. Greenblatt argues that the epideictic genre "is a received collective practice, but the social conditions of this practice—both the circumstances that make the genre possible and the objects that the genre represents—may change in such a way as to undermine the form" (101). Received collective practice in the epideictic genre from post-sophistic antiquity to twentieth century modernity has privileged homologous, monologic, logocentric praise-and-blame discourse. As Lyotard points out in *The Differend,* "a genre of discourse imprints a unique finality onto a multiplicity of heterogeneous phrases" (129): a genre silences polyphony and foregrounds a single dominant voice. The epideictic genre, as practiced in postsophistic and prepostmodern cultures, functions to subsume heterogeneous discourses into a single (universal, master, grand) narrative legitimating the social praxis of a dominant culture. In the late twentieth century, however, theories of postmodern culture have rendered untenable traditional Aristotelian praise-and-blame conceptions of epideictic rhetoric, creating an exigency for this rhetorical category to be transformed once more. Epideictic rhetoric has "traveled," Edward Said would say, into postmodernity, but we have not yet adequately theorized its new character or its new function in postmodern culture. I argue that epideictic rhetoric in postmodernity has turned away from its Aristotelian characterization as praise-and-blame discourse, has (re)turned to its pregeneric, subversive, sophistic "point of origin" and has transformed (in the process of its journey) into *graffitic immemorial discourse.*

The Greek noun *epideixis* has lived a complicated and politically charged semantic life. In its earliest usages, *epideixis* refers to any exhibition, display, or demonstration, whether rhetorical or otherwise. During the fifth century BCE, *epideixis* came to designate certain kinds of discourse: public discourse (as opposed to private discourse), display discourse (as opposed to pragmatic discourse). And in the third century BCE, Aristotle in the *Rhetoric* technologized *epideixis* into what many modern scholars now think of as epideictic rhetoric, revising earlier (sophistic) conceptions of epideictic rhetoric in two ways: first, he removed its sense of opposition to dialectic (1354a), thereby also eliminating its opposition to private and pragmatic discourse; and second, he endowed it with the status of genre (1358a–b).

In the *Rhetoric,* the noun *epideixis* becomes an adjective *epideiktikos* modifying *logos* (one of Aristotle's God words) and is deemed one of the three master rhetorical genres: deliberative rhetoric *(symbouleutikos logos),* judicial rhetoric *(dikanikos logos),* and demonstrative or epideictic rhetoric *(epideiktikos logos).* The points of reference for praising and blaming in Aristotle's epideictic genre are virtue (justice, courage, self-control, magnificence, magnanimity, liberality, gentleness, prudence, wisdom), vice (injustice, cowardice, lack of control, illiberality, little-mindedness, stinginess), the honorable (things productive of virtue, things brought about by virtue), and the shameful (things productive of vice, things brought about by vice) (1.9.1–27). Aristotle divides epideictic discourse that praises virtue and honor into *epainos* (praise of a subject's inherent virtue or ethos) and *enkomium* (praise of a subject's actions) (1.9.33); and the characteristics of *psogos*, epideictic discourse that criticizes (or blames) vice and shamefulness, may be derived through opposition to the characteristics of *epainos* and *enkomium* (1.9.41).

As Berlin points out in "Aristotle's Rhetoric in Context," these objects of praise and blame in epideictic rhetoric are clear markers of class distinction: magnanimity and liberality are possible only for wealthy land owners; and justice, prudence, and wisdom come with appropriate civic education, a luxury of the leisure classes (55–64). The social function of Aristotelian epideictic rhetoric is to subsume the contradictions of material-lived culture into a hegemonic grand narrative of proper civic behavior, constructing and maintaining ruling-class social dominance. As Aristotle points out, persuasive proofs are not necessary in epideictic discourse since its audience does not question the truth value of the orator's claims: "The facts need to be taken on trust, and speakers rarely introduce evidence of them" (3.17.3). Audiences, in other words, uncritically accommodate into their own public and private cultural practices the values expressed in epideictic discourse. As Aristotle puts it, the epideictic orator "should make the hearer think he shares the praise" (3.14.11). The virtues praised, however, are those of the ruling class. Through the amplification of communally accepted norms for behavior—that is, the norms of the dominant class—and through idealizing real events, epideictic rhetoric functions to maintain hegemonic power formations and repress the desire for liberation among marginalized classes; it weaves status quo power relations into the very cultural fabric of society.

Because sophistic epideictic rhetoric is most commonly described merely as display rhetoric composed for general public consumption (Chase 293, Guthrie 41–44), following Aristotle's lead, its real subversive potential and its reliance on the unique exigencies of individual rhetorical situations are often obscured. However, Takis Poulakos notes that classical epideictic rhetoric "discloses the capacity that participants of a society have to become social agents by articulating their own versions of the social order." Epideictic oratory, in other words, represents, always in politicized language, *perceived* values; and rhetors of any cultural group have the potential, realized or not, to represent social values as they perceive them, whatever the *status quo*. Poulakos continues:

> Conceived as the site of a critique or transformation of the
> social order, the genre of epideictic oratory can no longer be
> understood as a stable ground upon which tradition leaves
> its unalterable traces and attains an intelligibility that persists
> across time. Rather, the totality of works that make up the
> tradition of epideictic oratory must be understood as a his-
> torical register that supplies us with a heritage of conflicting
> valuations among participants of various societies at various
> times. In this way, the act of interpretation . . . provides an
> occasion for inquiring into conflicts and struggles over the
> contestation of specific values in specific societies. ("Cul-
> tural" 161)

Epideictic rhetoric does not always represent dominant values; in sub-
cultural contexts, the possibility of promoting subversive values always
exists. And as Theodor W. Adorno has said, "Steady drops hollow the
stone" (134).

Scott Consigny suggests that "Gorgias uses the epideictic as an instrument to challenge the foundationalist assumptions of his audience"
("Sophistic Challenges" 110), a far cry from Aristotle's description of
epideictic rhetoric as uncontested dominant discourse. Consigny continues:

> In each of his four extant [epideictic] works, Gorgias . . .
> induces a "crisis of reason" for his audience, exposing the
> inherent limits and inadequacy of their privileged *logos,* and
> requiring them to confront the immediate crisis in a new way.
> In these works, he in effect holds a mirror up to the audience
> itself rather than to "nature," displaying the arbitrariness of
> their own *logos* and the ways in which they are deceived by
> it. (113)

Takis Poulakos agrees that sophistic epideictic oratory undermines status quo discourse "from within," suggesting that in Gorgias's *Epitaphios*
(or funeral oration), the sophist uses the very formal properties of the
genre itself to critique the "institutional practices" he inherited ("Historical" 91).

In addition to their potentially subversive quality, sophistic epideictic
speeches were also written and delivered in a variety of rhetorical situations; thus, the sociopolitical contexts of delivery determined their
meaning as much as their referential content. As Consigny points out:

> Gorgias appears to violate conventional criteria used to as-
> sess reasoning and style in his epideictic orations because the
> skill he exhibits is one of prevailing in diverse discourses, each
> possessing its own protocols of reasoning and style. Rather
> than adhering to universal criteria, Gorgias suggests that the
> criteria for assessing reasoning and style are relative to spe-
> cific, arbitrarily accepted discourses of the culture. ("Gorgias's
> Use" 283)

One of the central themes throughout Gorgias's writings is the ancient
notion of *kairos,* the right or opportune moment. Prior to Gorgias, the
term *kairos* was applied to the weaver's ability to thrust a thread through
a momentary opening in the loom and the archer's ability to exploit the
minuscule opening in space that would guide an arrow to its target.
However, Gorgias, departing from his predecessors, applied this useful
concept to *logos,* constructing in the process a doctrine of rhetorical
context (Consigny, "Gorgias's Use" 284–85).

Postmodern epideictic rhetoric, like sophistic epideictic rhetoric, is
graffitic because its signs derive meaning as much from their sociotextual
contexts as from their referential content; and, like sophistic epideictic
rhetoric, postmodern epideictic rhetoric is *immemorial* because its primary goal is to subvert dominant-class hegemonic discourse. In *Heidegger and "the jews,"* Lyotard argues that a modernist (and Aristotelian) conception of epideictic rhetoric as praise-and-blame discourse
operates according to a "politics of forgetting" (4): "It requires the forgetting of that which may question the community and its legitimacy"
(7). The exigency that generates epideictic discourse, in other words,
signals a culture crisis. As Lyotard puts it, "The pain brought on by
shame and by doubt generates the edification of the worthy, the certain,
the noble, and the just" (8). Postmodern epideictic rhetoric (graffitic
immemorial discourse), on the other hand, does not praise the socially
constructed virtues that characterize a ruling class ideology or criticize
(blame) the vices that work against that ideology; instead, graffitic immemorial discourse represents what has been left unrepresented (what
has been repressed by the hegemonic logics of dominant-class ideologies), counter-representing memorialized representations, creating subversive memorials and immemorial subversions; it shifts and fragments
sociotextual contexts, subversively placing dominant signs into contradictory settings and arranging contradictory dominant signs into subversive collages.

In postmodern epideictic rhetoric, graffitic signs comprise inter-(con)textually saturated graph(it)ic signifiers (graphic manifestations of graffitic immemorial discourse) at subversive play within host socio-textual contexts that infuse graph(it)ic signifiers with semantic energies. Graffitic signifieds do not exist; they are the elitist illusions of Enlightenment humanists. But even if graffitic signifieds were to exist, sociotextual host contexts would smother their potential to effect or affect meaning. "Every sign," according to Derrida,

> can be *cited,* put between quotation marks; in so doing it can break with every given context, engendering an infinity of new contexts in a manner which is absolutely illimitable. This does not mean that the mark [or graphic sign] is valid outside of a context, but on the contrary that there are only contexts without any center or absolute anchoring. ("Signature" 320)

The practice of postmodern epideictic rhetoric (graffitic immemorial discourse) is precisely this practice of citation or quotation, this practice of removing graph(it)ic signifiers from their existing contexts and inserting them into alternative, subversive contexts. Postmodern epideictic rhetoric constructs subversive meaning, challenging the "traditional wisdom" of hegemonic discourse, in two ways: first, by transplanting signifiers into alternative contexts, subverting either the signifiers or the contexts or both; and second, by arranging signifiers into fragmented, oxymoronic collage-contexts, subverting by comparison each signifier's claim to Truth.

Most of us are familiar with the different manifestations of the Christian symbol of the fish, which often contains a cross or the word "Jesus" or the Greek word "ΙΧΘΥΣ" within its body. The symbol of the fish became associated with Christianity, and with Christ in particular, during the first two centuries of the Common Era, and the Greek word for fish ΙΧΘΥΣ became viewed as an anagram of Ιησους Χριστος Θεον Υιος Σωτηρ, which roughly translates "Jesus Christ, Son of God, Savior." But when the creation/evolution debates began to escalate as a result of some highly publicized trials involving public-school curricula, evolutionists used postmodern epideictic rhetoric (graffitic immemorial discourse) as a public way to subvert the creationist position. Evolutionists reproduced the Christian fish as a recognizable symbol but added legs to it and replaced the words "Jesus" and "ΙΧΘΥΣ" with the word "Darwin." Instead of a direct counterargument, in other words, evolutionists combined this Christian symbol with one of the primary signifiers of evolution ("Darwin"), thereby subverting the Christian use of the symbol of the fish and incorporating it into their own ideological framework. However, the creationists have had the last say (at least as far as I have seen), for they have constructed two more images that subvert the evolutionists' subversion of the Christian fish symbol. The first shows a tombstone with an image of the legged "Darwin" fish lying upside down, and the caption reads, "Right now even Darwin is convinced." The second shows the legged "Darwin" fish swimming into the open mouth of a much larger fish with the word "TRUTH" inscribed in its body. Again, instead of direct counter arguments, creationists reclaimed their own symbol by subverting the evolutionists' subversion of it, and this is the very kind of subversion that is characteristic of the first variety of postmodern epideictic rhetoric.

Some uses of collage can also be forms of graffitic immemorial discourse, and they usually fall into the second category of postmodern epideictic rhetoric. Each year at Purdue University, a number of female students compete to become homecoming queen. Part of this competition includes hanging poster-sized photographs of the women in the windows of private businesses and on bulletin boards throughout West Lafayette, Indiana. These posters permeate the entire Purdue campus and surrounding town, and students often boycott businesses that do not participate in this annual two-dimensional display of feminine pulchritude. According to the dominant logic that endorses the contest, each poster of a homecoming queen candidate re-presents physical beauty; the photographs are signifiers of beautiful female signifieds. Each year, however, the Lafayette Discount Den (a small retail store that sells CDs, candy, and toiletries) uses postmodern epideictic rhetoric (graffitic immemorial discourse) in the form of collage as a method of subverting this annual practice. Every fall semester, the Lafayette Discount Den creates a collage from the available posters of homecoming queen candidates: the collage itself is a compilation of body parts from a dozen or so different posters (one woman's nose, another's mouth, another's neck, two different eyes, two different ears, two different cheeks, and a hideous combination of all their hair). The Lafayette Discount Den neither praises the virtues of modesty nor blames the practice of displaying women's bodies in public spaces for contributing to patriarchal values. Instead, it chooses to participate in this annual practice for the purpose of subverting it. The creators of the annual collages take the most beautiful graph(it)ic signifiers (that is, the most beautiful physical features) from several posters and compile them into one grotesquely fragmented graph(it)ic signifier with no identifiable referent, no discernible graffitic signified.

Aristotelian praise-and-blame discourse, generated in accordance with dominant-class ideologies and uncritically accommodated by passive audiences, is no longer the predominant rhetorical mode of cultural production in postmodernity. Since the Vietnam War, postmodern epideictic rhetoric (graffitic immemorial discourse), generated from multiple political subjectivities, produces culture through subversive semiotics. Given the prominent role that postmodern epideictic rhetoric plays in contemporary discourse (especially the media), it is vital to develop strategies for consuming and composing graffitic immemorial discourse, and the most effective resource we have for accomplishing this task is cultural studies. Cultural studies comprises an interdisciplinary blend of critical strategies for examining everyday social practices as they occur within specific social, economic, and political contexts; its practitioners seek to understand how social groups and institutions produce culture (through politicized representations), consume culture (from multiple and contradictory subject positions), and distribute the culture they produce (according to socially constructed localized modes of legitimation). In "Encoding/Decoding," Stuart Hall argues that we need not accommodate as passive subjects the dominant discourses that interpellate us; we must learn also to negotiate and resist these discourses and produce alternative discourses that subvert dominant ones and open possibilities for more egalitarian social formations. Those who are able to negotiate or resist dominant hegemonic graph(it)ic signifiers and are able to compose subversive graph(it)ic signifiers will exercise a degree of control over their cultural lives that they might otherwise lack. Through cultural studies, then, we can develop and occupy powerfully critical subject positions from which to consume and compose postmodern epideictic rhetoric (graffitic immemorial discourse).

5
The Global Village, Multiculturalism, and the Functions of Sophistic Rhetoric

In his final and most generative work, *Rhetorics, Poetics, and Cultures,* James A. Berlin argues that theories and practices of rhetoric are both the products and producers of particular economic, political, and social conditions. I accept Berlin's premise as axiomatic; and thus I begin this final chapter's journey into rhetoric with the following question: If we agree (though certainly not all of us will) that our present and future economic, political, and social conditions may generally be described as a global village, then how *do, will,* and *should* the conditions of globalization affect our present and future theories and practices of rhetoric? Later in this chapter, I argue that the sophistic, particularly Gorgianic doctrine of *kairos* (the right moment) is an effective strategy for harnessing the competing discourses that characterize communication in the global village.

Before anything else, though, we must ask, "What is the 'global village'?" The global village is a real and imagined space, a contact zone in which, by virtue of radical advancements in travel and communication technologies, different cultures encounter each other. The global village is real because certain transformations of our material existence are, in fact, bringing disparate, once-isolated cultures into contact; it is imagined because cultural theorists, many of whom are mentioned below, describe the global village in differently inflected ways. Some of the material transformations that have piqued interest in the global village are startling. The technologies of air travel, for example, have improved so much in such little time that many who were born near the turn of the twentieth century witnessed the first flights at Kitty Hawk (1903), the first transatlantic flight from the U.S. to Ireland (1919), the first supersonic flight (1947), and the first human space flights (1961)—all within less than 60 years of their own lifetimes. Communication technologies, too, have improved exponentially in just a few decades. Although the telephone and radio were in use shortly before and after the turn of the century, the television was not widely available until after World War II. More startling, computers, invented in the 1930s and 1940s, were not available for general public use until the 1970s, when the first microcomputers, word processors, and related software were introduced. Although the first networked email system, ARPANET, was invented in the 1960s, the Internet and the World Wide Web were not in common use until the late 1980s and 1990s. These dramatic improvements in travel and communication technologies have given rise to a "contact zone" of *global* proportions. Mary Louise Pratt defines a "contact zone" as a "space in which peoples geographically and historically separated come into contact with each other and establish ongoing relations, usually involving conditions of coercion, radical inequality, and intractable conflict" (34). For good or ill, a global contact zone *exists* and is *imagined* to exist in certain ways. According to Hisham M. Nazer, "When, for the first time, each and every culture is forced to take other cultures into account, even the most conservative commentator should not hesitate in calling this a watershed era in the lives of human beings" (6).

There have emerged at least four distinct positions in the discourse on the global village, each with its own unique virtues and difficulties. First, there are scholars who argue that the theory of the global village is largely a myth, an exaggerated rumor, wishful thinking. Paul Hurst and Grahame Thompson, for example, believe that the process of international trade has in no way resulted in a globalized culture, and those who imagine the so-called global village do so for unrealistic and utopian purposes. Of course, such a position, focused as it is on denial, threatens to leave the very real phenomenon of globalization to evolve unchecked, dominated by whoever has the knowledge and capital to control it.

Second, other scholars welcome the arrival of the global village with open arms, believing that this utopian "space" is not only the result of shifts in communication technologies and multicultural interaction but also the reflection of human cognitive evolution. Marshal McLuhan and Bruce Powers, for example, view the global village as the material result of a technology-induced shift in the very cognitive processes of human thought from left-brain dominance to right-brain dominance. The obvious problem with the cognitive evolution position, however, is that McLuhan and Powers naïvely ignore the Western and capitalist political projects of those who create and control the media technologies with this awesome power to alter human consciousness. Nazer, for example, accepts McLuhan and Powers's thesis, yet he describes globalization as a potentially sinister process:

> The consciousness of people in the age of the Internet and global communications has become a human project, a target for those who wish to impose a universal [that is, Western] vision on a totally penetrated, utterly non-insular world. The central thrust of this [largely capitalist project] will be to enter the subjectivity of other human beings through the use of technology and the projection of mobilized meaning through symbols and images. As this technological expansion goes forward and the human systems for using it become more sophisticated, a power will be realized that will, in time, transcend military and economic leverage. (xiv)

For Nazer, then, there *is* a cognitive shift occurring in the process of globalization, but it is an insidious shift toward Western universalism and not toward some more creative capacity, as McLuhan and Powers believe.

Third, still other scholars view the global village with a certain ambivalence as a multicultural reality that must be addressed with specific strategies for intercultural communication. Riall W. Nolan summarizes this position:

> Globalization, as we're finding out, does not at all imply homogenization; quite the reverse. It means that we now have to deal with diversity directly, instead of at a distance. . . . Whether we see ourselves as competitors or collaborators in this new global environment, we are generally ill equipped for the demands it will make on us. (1)

Others view this global multicultural reality as an opportunity to learn and grow through cultural interaction, leading to more democratic and humane power structures around the world. For the most part, the scholars within this uncritical multicultural approach to the global village propose intercultural communication strategies that are intended to foster peace among disparate people (Nolan and Barnlund). However, as Ien Ang points out, the "existence of diversity" is in no way whatsoever "evidence of freedom from power and domination" (202). Further, there are a few, including Joseph J. DiStephano, Melvin Schnapper, Edward T. Hall, and Mildred Reed Hall, who adapt intercultural communication strategies for use in characteristically Western capitalist pursuits. Hall and Hall, for example, describe communication strategies for *American*-based multinational corporations (that is, those producing Western cultural artifacts for *general* consumption) that would benefit from a structural understanding of foreign cultures, and DiStephano and Schnapper focus on providing corporate managers with intercultural communication skills that will help them succeed in the global marketplace.

Finally, some scholars such as Peter Golding, Nazer, John Tomlinson, and Vasily Vakhrushev contend that the global village is nothing less than a high-tech form of capitalist, hegemonic neocolonialism. Golding argues:

> The arrival of new communication and information technologies has offered the promise of more egalitarian, participatory, and progressive structures. Yet in practice, the reality has been of their rapid incorporation into familiar structures of inequity and commercial exploitation. (79)

While Golding laments that technology has failed to produce new, more democratic power formations, Vakhrushev and Nazer argue that technology has indeed produced new power formations—universalizing, colonializing formations with the interest of only a few influential institutions in mind. According to Nazer:

> By controlling global communications and international institutions, certain Western notions can now penetrate all [other] cultures and nations. If successful in this effort, the relationship between nations [regardless of their cultural origins] will be entirely Western in construction. (4)

Further, "the prize they win will be the ability to define 'appropriate' and 'acceptable' actions among world nations to fit Western political and economic agendas" (8). If, as Benedict Anderson contends, nations and communities are imagined, then this newly *imagined* global community benefits only the leaders of Western industry and colonizes everyone else.[1] Two scholars in particular take a negotiated stance within this neocolonialism position: David Morley and Kevin Robins agree that globalization can have negative, colonializing effects; however, they also view it as a potential resource for the reassertion of localized discourses in non-Western communities.

My own view of the global village combines elements of all of these positions. With Hurst and Thompson, I consider *the* global village, as many describe it, to be an unachievable, mythic, imagined place; I believe with Nazer and McLuhan and Powers that human interaction with new technologies necessarily changes human thought processes; I concur with Nolan and Barnlund that the global village is a multicultural reality (in the sense of a reality that has both a material and an imagined existence) that must be addressed with specific strategies for intercultural communication; and finally, with Vakhrushev, Golding, and, again, Nazer, I also see vast potential, especially through computer technologies, for a few to gain tremendous economic, cultural, social, and political power over many others. Needless to say, what interests me here is how communication operates (and should operate) in this complex present and future world.

Rhetoric and Communication in the Global Village

Rhetoric and communication are at the very heart of the global village; put another way, the global village is all about communication. According to Robert W. McChesney:

> Communication is directly implicated in the "globalization" process in at least two ways. First, due in part to stunning developments such as digital and satellite communication technologies, communication and information are coming to play a larger and more important role in capitalist economies. To the extent globalization does exist as an economic process, it is based to no small extent on the rise of rapid global communication networks. Some even go so far as to argue that "information" has replaced manufacturing as the foundation of the economy. Second, the commercial media, advertising, and telecommunication markets themselves are rapidly globalizing, arguably even more so than the balance of the political economy. Indeed, global media and communication are in some respects the advancing armies of global capitalism. (2)

When people of disparate cultures are forced to interact and when the very technological means by which communication takes place evolve at a dizzying pace, our traditional, linear models of communication necessarily break down. Within the rhetorical context of this global village, then, we are forced to rethink how different people interact through audial, textual, and visual symbols. In the global village, the exigencies for our own messages may be clear to us, but the cultural backgrounds of our interlocutors and the technological means for communicating with them remain utterly uncertain. Thus, in order for successful communication to occur in this global contact zone (of course, different cultures define success in different ways), communication must be able to accommodate any new situation that might arise; it must be able to adapt to audiences, subject matters, and material, social, and institutional contexts that were previously unknown, never before encountered.

In *The Global Village*, McLuhan and Powers argue that our twentieth-century, high-tech telecommunications and high-speed modes of travel have linked once disparate and isolated cultures into a single unit, and this global village requires new approaches to social understanding and communication, for "when no provision is made for two entirely different points of view, the result is violence. One person or another loses his identity" (ix–x). Yet when different points of view are considered in the communication process, the problem of uncertainty is multiplied. McLuhan and Powers suggest that "whenever two cultures, or two events, or two ideas are set in proximity to one another, an interplay takes place, a sort of magical change. The more unlike the interface, the greater the tension in the interchange" (4). While culture clash is one major defining characteristic of the global village, the clash between humans and new technologies is equally important. According to McLuhan and Powers:

> Electronic man, having found himself in an arena of simultaneous information, also finds himself increasingly excluded from the older more traditional (visual) world in which shape and reason seem to be uniform, connected, and stable. Instead Western (visual and sequential) man now discovers himself habitually relating to information structures which are simultaneous, discontinuous, and dynamic. He has been plunged into a new form of knowing, far from his customary experience tied to the printed page. (18)

For McLuhan and Powers, new technologies do not just influence human communication—they transform the very humans who communicate: "Technologies involve the transformation of the user insofar as they establish new relationships between him and his environments" (8), and "when media work together they can so change our consciousness as to create whole new universes of psychic meaning" (87). Computer technologies more than any other have caused a kind of biological paradigm shift in human thought processes—from left-brain to right-brain dominance (103); and the "ultimate interactive nature of some video-related technologies will produce the dominant right-hemisphere social patterns of the next century" (83). Indeed, McLuhan and Powers predict that

> The United States by [the year] 2020 will achieve a distinct psychological shift from a dependence on visual, uniform, homogenous thinking, of a left-hemisphere variety, to a multi-faceted configurational mentality, . . . [or] right-hemisphere thinking. In other words, instead of being captured by point-to-point linear attitudes, so helpful to the mathematician and accountant, most Americans will be able to tolerate many different thought systems at once, some based on antagonistic ethnic heritages. Social patterns will have more weight than alphanumeric measurements. (86)

One solution to this radical uncertainty, both cultural and technological, lies in understanding the influence technologies have on human thought processes, and, according to McLuhan and Powers, we can accomplish this goal by applying the Gestalt theory of "figure" and "ground" to the various technologies of communication as they emerge and evolve: "All cultural situations are composed of an area of attention (figure) and a very much larger area of inattention (ground)" (5). Further,

> In the order of things, ground comes first. The figures arrive later. Coming events cast their shadows before them. The ground of any technology is both the ground that gives rise to it as well as the whole environment (medium) of services and disservices that the technology brings with it. These are the side effects, and they impose themselves haphazardly as a new form of culture. The medium is the message. As an old ground is displaced by the content of a new situation, it becomes available to ordinary attention as figure. (6)

For most individuals, the technology itself (as figure) is in clear focus, but the culture of that technology (as ground) is hidden; however, a full understanding of the ways in which technology influences human communication requires an understanding of this hidden cultural environment, and we can accomplish this goal through relating new technologies (new figures) that are available for analysis to familiar cultural contexts (contexts or grounds that have already been displaced).

By comparing new technologies to prior (now visible) contexts, we are able to shed light on the *present* (once invisible) context, and McLuhan and Powers offer the tetrad, a four-question heuristic, as a powerful method for analyzing hidden cultural contexts. The four questions of the tetrad, which I have paraphrased in the interest of brevity, are:

1. What does any new artifact/technology (figure) enlarge or *enhance* from previous contexts (grounds)?
2. What does it erode or *obsolesce?*
3. What does it *retrieve* that had been earlier obsolesced?
4. What does it *reverse* or flip into when pushed to the limits of its potential? (9)

According to McLuhan and Powers, "the tetrad . . . helps us to see both figure and ground at a time when the latent effects of the mechanical age tend to obscure the ground subliminally. Its chief utility is that it raises the hidden ground to visibility" (9). Thus, McLuhan and Powers locate the radical uncertainty that characterizes global village communication in the subliminal, obscure context or ground—that is, the very situation in which rhetorical interaction takes place—yet they offer the tetrad as "an instrument for revealing and predicting the dynamics of innovations and new situations" (18).

McLuhan and Powers contend that "nothing has meaning except in relation to the environment, medium, or context that contains it" (71), and the tetrad is one way to illuminate uncertain contexts:

In presenting the perceptual patterns of the tetrad form, the object is to draw attention to situations that are still in process, situations that are structuring new perceptions and shaping new environments, even while they are restructuring old ones, so that it might be said that structures of media dynamics are inseparable from performance. The effort is always to draw attention to the laws of composition as well as to the factors of regulation and interplay. (28)

And once we have brought uncertainty to light, we understand that our traditional notion of time, as a continuous and linear progression *(chronos)*, is insufficient, since only certainty marches forward in a predictable path; we must now articulate a different sense of time, a qualitative sense of time, one that is able to account for the historical "ruptures" (borrowing a term from Foucault) that result from diversity and uncertainty. As we have already seen, the ancients called this qualitative sense of time *kairos.*

Despite all their talk of diversity and uncertainty, which I have highlighted throughout my discussion, McLuhan and Powers do unnecessarily slip into occasional universalizing discourse, as when they make claims like the following: "The media extensions of man are the *homogenization* of the planet" (93, my emphasis), and "The computer is the first component of that hybrid of video-related technologies which will move us toward a *world consciousness*" (103, my emphasis). McLuhan and Powers, on occasion, describe the global village as a structural foundation (a place) with certain characteristics. But this structural foundation, this utopian place, this universal global village is a problematic construction. When we talk about *the* global village as a structure (a "homogenization," a "world consciousness") to be achieved by a certain date, the year 2020, for example, we generalize its nature and function beyond its actual scope. Describing the global village as an achievable structure can neither account for how individuals and communities perceive and use technology nor can it account for how technology impacts the modes of thought (right-hemisphere dominance, left-hemisphere dominance) that individuals and communities enact in the practice of everyday life. It is only this universalizing aspect of McLuhan and Powers's theory of the global village to which I take exception, but it is also with this infrequent utopian desire that many recent critics of McLuhan and Powers have been most concerned.

The problem with universalizing and utopian images of the global village (a discourse in which McLuhan and Powers do occasionally engage, as well as many who occupy the uncritical multicultural position described above) is, according to Ien Ang, that it "implies the progressive homogenization—through successful communication—of the world as a whole" (194). Ang contends that "McLuhan's 'global village,' a world turned into a single community through the annihilation of space in time, represents nothing other than (the fantasy of) the universal culmination of capitalist modernity" (195). Since much of Ang's discussion of communication in the global village is predicated on this critique of McLuhan (and Powers), I feel compelled to clarify my position on the matter: I agree with Ang's critique of universalizing and utopian treatments of the global village, yet I must point out again that this kind of discourse is *infrequent* (though certainly present at times) throughout McLuhan and Powers's discussion. Thus, while I accept Ang's arguments as a whole, some of which are summarized here, I believe his critique of McLuhan (and Powers) is somewhat misplaced and exaggerated.

According to Ang, our traditional transmission models of communication are sufficient only to explain how language has been used by capitalist and modernist cultures as a tool for social control; they are insufficient to account for the uncertainty that characterizes the global village.

> The control effected by communication-as-transmission does not only pertain to the conquest of markets for the benefit of economic gain; it is also a control over people. In social terms, then, communication-as-transmission has generally implied a concern with social order and social management, . . . an (unstated) desire for a disciplined population and therefore a belief in the possibility of an ordered and stable "society" [where] social integration (e.g. through the dissemination of a "central value system" throughout the entire social fabric) is the main concern. . . . Here, the making of the "global village" can be rewritten as the transformation, or domestication, of non-Western Others in the name of capitalist modernity, the civilization which was presumed to be the universal destiny of humankind: global spatial integration is equated with global social and cultural integration.
>
> It should be clear that in theoretical terms transmission models of communication inherently privilege the position of the Sender as legitimate source and originator of meaning and action, the centre from which both spatial and social/cultural integration is effectuated. Communication is deemed successful if and when the intentions of the Sender, packaged in the Message, arrive unscathed at the Receiver, sorting the intended effects. (195)

But Ang contends that "the hegemony of such linear and transparent conceptions of communication has been severely eroded in the last few decades" (195), on both political and epistemological grounds, by the *uncertainty* that characterizes the global village. According to Ang:

> It should surprise no one that the transmission paradigm was particularly pervasive in communication theory during the

high period of American hegemony as the superpower within the modern capitalist world. Neither is it surprising that the crisis of the paradigm erupted when that hegemony started to display cracks and fissures. (197)

Ang argues that if rhetoric and communication are to take full account of the "postmodern uncertainty" characteristic of the global village, then "it is the *failure* of communication that we should emphasize" (198), not its "successful" (and thereby oppressive) transmission.

> What needs to be stressed is the fundamental *uncertainty* that necessarily goes with the process of constructing a meaningful order, the fact that communicative practices do not necessarily arrive at common meanings at all. . . . [A] radically semiotic perspective ultimately subverts the concern with (successful) communication by foregrounding the idea of "no necessary correspondence" between the Sender's and the Receiver's meanings. That is to say, not success, but failure to communicate should be considered "normal" in a cultural universe where commonality of meaning cannot be taken for granted. . . . If the Sender's intended message does not "get across," this is not a "failure in communications" resulting from unfortunate "noise" or the Receiver's misinterpretation, but because the Receiver's active participation in the construction of meaning doesn't take place in the same ritual order as the Sender's. . . . [Thus,] it is precisely the existence of correspondence and commonality of meaning, not its absence, which needs to be accounted for. (Ang 198)

Yet, Ang continues, "postmodern uncertainty" does not result in a radical form of chaos: "If the forces of order are continuously deployed without ever achieving complete order, then the forces of chaos are also continuously impinging on the system without ever resulting in total chaos." This double pressure—of system and chaos—creates a culture whose "hegemony rests on the setting of structural limits, themselves precarious, to the possibilities of random excess" (209), and the "unstable multiplicity of this system" (that is, its chaos-within-limits) "no longer makes it possible, as modern discourse would have it, to tell a single, total story about the world 'today'" (211). There is, in other words, no single, universalizing, totalizing, utopian narrative about the process or structure of the global village. The fundamental problem with Ang's discussion, however, is that it achieves nothing more than a negative dialectic, a refutation of everything known, yet it neglects to describe or even point toward the possibility of a theory or practice of rhetoric within this global world of uncertainty.

I prefer to view the global village neither as a structure to be achieved (as McLuhan and Powers occasionally view it) nor as a liberal, grand narrative (as many of the uncritical multiculturalists discussed above view it); rather, I prefer to view the global village as a *heuristic* with which to explore the process of culture as it is lived. The global village, or more accurately the process of globalization, is not a structure or a place but a discursive practice, a collection of universalizing rhetorical "strategies" to which individuals and communities may respond with "tactics" designed to negotiate globalizing rhetoric from local perspectives. I borrow these two terms, strategies and tactics, from Michel de Certeau's *The Practice of Everyday Life,* and it is in their contradistinction that I believe we can find a *useful* model for communication within the complex discursive process of globalization.

Rhetorical Strategies and Tactics: *Kairos* in Practice

In *The Practice of Everyday Life,* de Certeau describes strategies and tactics as a kind of dialectical power struggle at the level of discourse. A strategy, according to de Certeau, is

> the calculation (or manipulation) of power relationships that becomes possible as soon as a subject with will and power (a business, an army, a city, a scientific institution) can be isolated. It postulates a place that can be delimited as its *own* and serve as the base from which relations with an exteriority composed of targets or threats (customers or competitors, enemies, the country surrounding the city, objectives and objects of research, etc.) can be managed. As in management, every "strategic" rationalization seeks first of all to distinguish its "own" place, that is, the place of its own power and will, from an "environment." . . . [I]t is an effort to delimit one's own place in a world bewitched by the invisible powers of the Other. It is also the typical attitude of modern science, politics, and military strategy. (35–36)

The manifestations of these "calculations of power relationships," these "places of power" (as opposed to real "environments"), take their ultimate shape in the discursive process of globalization—they are the globalizing discourses that seek structure and order.

Tactics, on the other hand, are those discourses that emerge when strategies, which inevitably serve the economic, social, and political interests of a few powerful groups backed by even more-powerful institutions, are recognized as oppressive by those whom the strategies work to control. A tactic, de Certeau explains,

> is a calculated action determined by the absence of a proper locus. No delimitation of an exteriority, then, provides it with the condition necessary for autonomy. The space of a tactic is the space of the other. Thus it must play on and with a terrain imposed on it and organized by the law of a foreign power. It does not have the means to *keep to itself,* at a distance, in a position of withdrawal, foresight, and self-collection; it is a maneuver . . . within enemy territory. It does not, therefore, have the options of planning general strategy and viewing the adversary as a whole within a distinct, visible, and objectifiable space. It operates in isolated actions, blow by blow. It takes advantage of "opportunities" and depends on them, being without any base where it could stockpile its winnings, build up its own position, and plan raids. What it wins it cannot keep. This nowhereness gives a tactic mobility, to be sure, but a mobility that must accept the chance offerings of the moment, and seize on the wing the possibilities that offer themselves at any given moment. It must vigilantly make use of the cracks that particular conjunctions open in the surveillance of the proprietary powers. It poaches in them. It creates surprises in them. It can be where it is least expected. It is a guileful ruse. (*Practice* 36–37)

Tactics are rhetorical practices that can work to subvert a dominant order while operating within the very order they mean to subvert. Tactics rely on "opportunities," "chance offerings of the moment," and "possibilities that offer themselves at any given moment." As rhetorical techniques, then, tactics draw their power not from a linear sense of time as progression, steady and predictable, but from a qualitative sense of time as opportunity, plagued by chance yet empowered by possibility. In tactics we see the workings of *kairos.*

Universalizing, essentialist, and utopian global village discourses are inevitable—they are inescapable; they are an inherent aspect of many of our most powerful social, economic, political, and cultural institutions. These are the strategies. And because strategies are universalizing, essentialist, and utopian, they are not consciously applied in situations but are assumed applicable to any circumstance. Yet I argue that what characterize intercultural communications within this context are the different ways in which communicators subvert and negotiate the discourses of globalization according to the exigencies of particular situations. These are the tactics, and tactics comprise the practice(s) of everyday life. Further, tactics are sophistic in nature, a point that de Certeau himself makes clear:

> In the enormous rhetorical corpus devoted to the art of speaking, the Sophists have a privileged place, from the point of view of tactics. The principle was, according to the Greek rhetorician Corax, to make the weaker position seem the stronger, and they claimed to have the power of turning the tables on the powerful by the way in which they made use of the opportunities offered by the particular situation. (*Practice* xx)

One of the earliest technologized aspects of the sophistic theories of rhetoric in the fifth century BCE was, according to Edward Schiappa, the conception of *kairos* (*Protagoras* 73).

Although there were no supersonic airplanes or telecommunication satellites to connect people in a flash during the fifth century BCE, there were, nonetheless, disparate cultures coming into continual contact in Periclean Athens through open, public discourse. According to Jacqueline de Romilly, countless sophists from the furthest reaches of the known world traveled to Periclean Athens. Athenians welcomed traveling professionals, allowing them to live and teach in the city for as long as they wished to do so. And these traveling sophists *wished* to live and teach in Athens, partly because of the wealth and prestige concentrated there from the city's military victories and also because Pericles had made Athens the embodiment of democratic ideals shared by many of the sophists. As I have already pointed out, the sophists in Athens were a diverse group, articulating disparate epistemologies and critiquing each other's methods for teaching rhetoric and other disciplines. Athens had become, by the mid-fifth century BCE, a concentrated contact zone in which culturally inflected ideas (originating from as far away as Asia, Italy, Egypt, and distant islands in the Mediterranean Sea) clashed in an unprecedented polylog. In Athens's fertile intellectual environment, the traveling sophists were free to explore ideas that might have resulted in banishment from other lands, because many (though certainly not all) of these ideas challenged oppressive oligarchic and monarchic power structures.

Gorgias came to Athens in 427 BCE as part of a Leontinian embassy seeking support in their civil war against Sicilian neighbor Syracuse. Syracuse, backed by the powerful Corinthians, fought hard to establish oligarchic rule throughout Sicily. Leontini, wishing to remain a democracy, received twenty war ships from Athens in 427 BCE and forty-five more in 425 BCE, allowing Leontini to stave off the advancing armies of Syracuse. In 422 BCE, however, civil war broke out in Leontini, leaving the democrats weakened, and soon Syracuse conquered the Leontinian democracy, establishing in its place a restricted oligarchy (Enos 9–11). It is not known in what year Gorgias returned to Athens as a permanent resident to teach and practice rhetoric; however, it was certainly not long after the embassy of 427 BCE and may have been around the time of the oligarchic overthrow of Leontinian democracy in 422 BCE. As I argued in chapter 1, Gorgias's most prominent rhetorical principle, the doctrine of seizing the right moment *(kairos)*, is incompatible with foundational epistemologies and their associated oligarchic forms of government. From the 420s BCE onward, the Gorgian *kairos* flourished in the fertile intellectual context of Athenian democracy.

Kairos—seizing the opportune moment, choosing arguments depending on the demands of the situation—was, according to Kinneavy, a prevalent concept in Greek thought from Hesiod through Plato, and it was also one of the fundamental tactics of certain sophists' rhetorical methods. Its function within the relativistic and democratic sophists' rhetorical arts was to confound powerful, perhaps even institutionalized, rhetorical strategies. Following is a selection of various sophistic and pre-Socratic treatments of *kairos*, all of which can be found in Hermann Diels and Walther Kranz's *Die Fragmente Der Vorsokratiker:*

Democritus:

- One must be on one's guard against the bad man, lest he seize his opportunity *[mê kairou labêtai]*. (Freeman, *Ancilla* B87)
- Freedom of speech is the sign of freedom; but the danger lies in discerning the right occasion *[hê tou kairou diagnôsis]*. (Freeman, *Ancilla* B226)

Anaxarchus:

- Much learning can help much, but also can greatly harm him who has it. It helps the clever man, but harms him who readily utters every word in any company. One must know the measure of the right time *[kairou metra]*, for this is the boundary of wisdom. Those who recite a saying outside the right time *[eksô kairou]*, even if their saying is wise, are reproached with folly, because they do not mix intelligence with wisdom. (Freeman, *Ancilla* B1)

Anonymous *Dissoi Logoi:*

- Quotes an anonymous poet: There is nothing that is in every respect seemly or shameful, but the right moment *[ho kairos]* takes the same things and makes them shameful and then changes them round and makes them seemly. (Robinson 2.19)
- Comments on the above quote: All things are seemly when done at the right moment *[kairôi]*, but shameful when done at the wrong moment *[akairiai]*. (Robinson 2.20)

There are, in other words, two preconditions for successful rhetoric: first, the rhetor must be free to speak, and second, the rhetor should possess knowledge of the subject. If the rhetor possesses these two preconditions, then the ultimate success of any rhetorical venture lies in seizing the right moments, the fleeting opportunities, since something said at the wrong time (or even something not said during a present opportunity) is a source of shame.

The doctrine of *kairos,* which had been in common circulation before the sophists, according to Mario Untersteiner, played a central role in Gorgias's rhetorical *technê.* However, although Untersteiner and even some ancient testimonia tell us that *kairos* was a fundamental aspect of Gorgianic rhetoric (and we have no epistemological or political reason to believe otherwise), the actual word *kairos* appears only once in Gorgias's extant texts. In the *Palamedes,* Gorgias's mythical character says, "Certainly it is not right for me to praise myself, but the present situation *[parôn kairos]* requires me to defend myself in every possible way since I have been accused of these crimes" (B11a.32). In other words, it is rarely the right moment for self praise; however, when faced with an untrue allegation that questions the character of the accused (as in Odysseus's allegation of treason against Palamedes), it *becomes* the right time by virtue of the situation to elevate one's own character. Thus, it is the rhetor's task to recognize and seize upon right moments as they arise.

But what force gives rise to a right moment for uttering certain arguments? For the answer to this question, we must turn to another term used by Gorgias, necessity *(anagkê)*, which precedes and supports the emergence of a right moment. Again in the *Palamedes*, Gorgias's mythical character says:

> For an accusation that is unsupported by proof causes confusion, and due to the present confusion [caused by Odysseus' unsupported allegation of treason], I am, of course, at a loss for words, unless I can invent some defense from the truth itself and the present necessity *[parousês anankês]*. (B11a.4)

Thus, it is the present necessity, the rhetorical context, that gives rise to the need to speak; it is the exigency of the situation that liberates and constrains the uses of particular arguments.

This description of *kairos* (and its precursor *anagkê*) resembles in many ways de Certeau's tactics; it speaks not of argument from institutional authority, not of an immutable base from which relations to others might be consistently managed; it speaks not a discourse of globalization, as Plato and others did, but a discourse of uncertainty, a discourse of tactics among powerful strategic discourses. Kairotic arguments do not dictate; they respond. When exploiting *kairos,* there is no steady locus of power, no universal strategy to follow; its operations are blow-by-blow, as fleeting as the right moment itself, taking advantage of opportunities as they arise. *Kairos,* then, as the concept was developed and inflected by the relativistic sophists in general and Gorgias in particular, remains a potent rhetorical tactic for harnessing the uncertainty of language and the contingency of situational contexts in the interest of democratic political and social ends.

Critical Multiculturalism and the Politics of *Kairos*

Twenty-four hundred years after the sophists, we see another arena in which the primary themes of this chapter—globalization, *kairos,* and rhetorical strategies and tactics—are thrust into the foreground, that is, in what we now call multiculturalism. Most multiculturalists view any form of globalizing as an invidious attempt to efface difference and exercise power, yet globalization is also an undeniable aspect of contemporary culture. Thus, if multicultural theory ignores or simplifies the process of globalization (as much of it does), focusing instead on the particulars of identity formation, then it weakens its own political veracity. Indeed, Jon Cruz urges us to "look at multiculturalism as part of a social logic of late capitalism and as a cultural feature at the intersec-

tion of economic globalization and the fiscal-domestic crisis of the state"
(19). During the 1960s and 1970s, according to Cruz, multiculturalists
in America made great strides in achieving new civil rights for oppressed
groups, and one reason for this (partial) success was their elevation of
the specific cultural values of oppressed cultures in *dialectical relation*
to existing national economic and cultural forces (28–30). However,
Cruz continues, "Just as the cultural dimensions of the state opened up
new spaces for raced and gendered identity formations" during this time,
"the fiscal crisis of the state began to register" as a force that would
subvert such identity formations. Centrifugal capitalism turned outward
"in search of transnational strategies" while centripetal culture "aug-
mented the process of identity formations" (28). And, according to Cruz,

> as the polity began to give racial groups the recognition of
> political subjects with civil rights, the economy began to move
> in directions that would quite quickly strip away the politi-
> cal resolve to underwrite this important cultural turn. As capi-
> talism began to spin centrifugally outward, dispersing and
> dispensing more and more of its material resources to main-
> tain *transnational trenches and alliances,* liberal democracy
> was challenged by conservative realignments, and in some
> spheres became increasingly frail, embattled, and brittle. (28)

Thus multiculturalism began turning away from its dreams of social reform toward the regressive formation of a new tribalism. Multiculturalism can only function as an effective discourse, Cruz concludes, if
it "operates simultaneously as *identity politics* and *sociosystemic politics.* Both are intimately intertwined" (33).

   Part of the reason for this new cultural tribalism in multicultural
theory is that multiculturalists themselves engage in a kind of internal
tribalism, unable to recognize the common project they once shared with
other multiculturalists. According to Cruz, multiculturalism has become
"an overloaded term, a symbolic container that is not capable of con-
taining the range of investments that it attempts to carry" (33), and it
does not take much study to discover the verity of Cruz's claim. A glance
through any anthology of multicultural theory reveals a proliferation of
subtheoretical camps: there are premodernist, modernist, postmodernist,
and antipostmodernist multiculturalists; there are conservative, corporate, and demagogic multiculturalists; there are antiracist, liberatory,
liberal, left-liberal, and managed multiculturalists; there are particular-

istic, pluralistic, polyvocal, polycentric, resistance, insurgent, and critical multiculturalists, among others. Most of these camps, however, were
either constructed as straw positions for generating counterarguments,
or they have fallen out of favor in recent articulations of multicultural
theory—except, that is, critical multiculturalism, the most promising site
for multicultural theory today. (Insurgent and polycentric multicul-
turalisms are *critical* in many ways and are sometimes included under
the more general heading of critical multiculturalism.)

One of the key concepts at the foundation of critical multiculturalism
as a theory and practice is the idea of hegemony. In the *Prison Notebooks,*
Antonio Gramsci describes hegemony in structuralist terms: it is a cultural condition in which, first, a dominator has power over a dominated,
and second, the dominated views the power exerted by the dominator
as natural, a universal and inalterable reality. However, in *Marxism and
Literature,* Raymond Williams incorporates a third element, an element
that turns hegemony from a structure into a process. According to Williams, not only is there domination that is viewed as natural, but there
must also be a perpetual process of consensus building:

> A lived hegemony is always a process. It is not, except ana-
> lytically, a system or structure. . . . Moreover, [hegemony]
> does not just passively exist as a form of dominance. It has
> continually to be renewed, re-created, defended, and modi-
> fied. It is also continually resisted, limited, altered, challenged
> by pressures not at all its own. We have to add to the con-
> cept of hegemony the concepts of counter-hegemony and
> alternative hegemony, which are real and persistent elements
> of practice. (112–13)

Hegemonic strategies and their opposition to alternative or counterhegemonic tactics comprise the process of social evolution, and since
cultures are processes not structures, the right timing of counterhegemonic discourse is crucial. If counterhegemonic cultures, misunderstand-
ing society as a structure not a process, employ universal (atemporal,
acontextual) strategies for inducing revolution, then dominant-hege-
monic forces will (as they have done for centuries) incorporate these
universal strategies into their own mechanisms for control, developing
an immunity to them and ensuring their future failure. However, when
counterhegemonic cultures use tactics that harness the power of the right
moment, that restrict their interventions to the specificity of particular

situational contexts, then dominant cultures cannot incorporate these tactics or become immune to their subversive power.

If we combine Gorgias, McLuhan, Gramsci, Williams, and de Certeau into a big pot of theory stew, we arrive at the following view of power: dominators establish globalizing strategies as a means to gain consensus among the dominated, and the dominated negotiate these strategies with timely, localized tactics as a means to gain control over their own lived experience. Critical multicultural theory in particular critiques the deployment of universalizing strategies and promotes the development of timely localizing tactics.

Critical multiculturalism fits in very well with this complex scheme of power and communication. Henry Giroux describes critical multiculturalism as "more than simply acknowledging differences and analyzing stereotypes; more fundamentally, it means understanding, engaging, and transforming the diverse histories, cultural narratives, representations, and institutions that produce racism and other forms of discrimination" (*Pedagogy* 237), all of which contribute to the hegemonic dominance of oppressed people; and in another context, Giroux argues that Gramsci's concept of hegemony should be central to any critical multicultural pedagogy (*Border* 186–88). According to Peter McLaren, the power structures that critical multiculturalism seeks to critique are maintained through the politics of signification: "Signs are part of an ideological struggle that attempts to create a particular regime of representation that serves to legitimate a certain cultural reality" (45), and "a critical multiculturalist curriculum can help teachers explore the ways in which students are differentially subjected to ideological inscriptions and multiply-organized discourses of desire through a politics of signification" (47).

However, while Giroux, McLaren, and many other critical multiculturalists have done much to develop pedagogies in which students critique dominant hegemonic culture and its globalizing representations, they have done little to help students develop specific rhetorical techniques that can chip away at the institutions that most affect their lives. They send students into battle with knowledge of the enemy but no ammunition. In other words, through critical multicultural pedagogies, students learn to critique structures of domination, but they learn no tactics of their own, no means to counter hegemonic structures. This deficiency in critical multicultural education is the result, I believe, of Giroux's, McLaren's, and others' reliance on Gramsci's inherently structuralist view of power, domination, and hegemony.

Multicultural rhetorical tactics may be either critical or productive, and both must be employed dialectically to maintain the health of diverse communities. Critical tactics are used to meet prejudice with resistance, and they rely on a conception of culture as a process, not a structure. For if culture is a process, then that process can be altered; but if it is a structure, then oppression is inevitable. Cultures evolve through the production of texts, and if enough subversive texts are entered into the flow of cultural production, then the culture itself will change gradually, incorporating subversive ideas into the very fabric of its own processes. Critical tactics, then, are aimed at subverting a dominant discourse. Productive tactics, on the other hand, are aimed at constructing communal subjectivities, as opposed to particular or universal subjectivities. Whereas critical tactics break down oppressive discourses, productive tactics construct communal, democratic, participatory discourses, providing a necessary base from which critique can proceed. Both critical and productive tactics are necessary, since critical tactics alone comprise only a negative dialectic with no articulated values of its own. Productive tactics construct those communal values and promote them in the face of oppressive discourses. Without the one, the other is senseless.

I argue that critical consciousness alone is not sufficient for citizens to participate in the formulation and reformulation of egalitarian power structures. We also need tactics, and we need to view hegemony not as a structure but as a process, not as an a priori formation but as a constant struggle. This is an inherently sophistic—and *neo*sophistic—view of social power. Understanding institutionalized strategies at any given point in time provides us with the discursive knowledge we need to compose our own *timely* rhetorical tactics, tactics that, a little at a time, work toward challenging marginalizing strategies. Adorno suggests that "steady drops hollow the stone" (134), and although sophistic "drops" may have been suppressed for many years, they are once again flowing, hollowing the stones of realism and foundationalism that stifle the most vital functions of rhetoric—its social functions. The study of individual texts or significations removed from institutional processes can help us develop critical sensibilities, but it does little to help us understand the shifting, temporal, discursive flow of institutional strategies (a kind of discursive *kairos*); and that, I argue, is where the real power of language is played out.

Appendix

Notes

Works Cited

Index

Appendix: A Selected Bibliography on Sophistic Rhetoric and Philosophy

This selected bibliography of sophistic scholarship in English since 1900 will, I hope, make the sophists more accessible to interested historians of rhetoric and philosophy. The sophists represented in this bibliography are those whose writings are translated in Rosamond Kent Sprague's edited collection of extant texts, *The Older Sophists*.

Because the sophists have been the subjects of many heated debates since Plato, I have used several criteria with which to limit the number of entries for this bibliography:

1. I omit sources that appeared before 1900, with a few notable exceptions by Edward Cope and Henry Sidgwick that I cite here:

> Cope, Edward M. "On the Sophistical Rhetoric." *Journal of Classical and Sacred Philology* 2 (1855): 129–69; and 3 (1856): 34–80, 253–88.
> ———. "The Sophists." *Journal of Classical and Sacred Philology* 1 (1854): 145–88.
> Sidgwick, Henry. "The Sophists." *Journal of Philology* 4 (1872): 288–307; and 5 (1874): 66–80.

These are certainly the most comprehensive treatments of sophistic doctrines before 1900, and they should not be overlooked.

2. I have restricted entries to those written in the English language even though much of the scholarship in sophistic studies appears in Italian and German. My purposes here are to make the sophists accessible to an English-speaking audience and to encourage English-language research on the sophists by scholars who may not have access to overseas journals.

3. Those numerous sources that treat the sophists solely as Plato presents them in his dialogues have been omitted. Because it is well known that Plato intentionally distorts sophistic teachings for his own purposes, I include only sources that discuss the sophistic texts in Sprague or Diels and Kranz.

4. Articles appearing in conference proceedings and festschrifts have been omitted. However, one particular volume of proceedings essays is especially useful and is frequently cited in English-language scholarship on the sophists. I cite it here:

Kerferd, G. B., ed. *The Sophists and Their Legacy.* Wiesbaden: Steiner, 1981.

Some of the sources listed in this bibliography are not easily categorized; thus a few are cited under multiple headings. In "Primary Sources" the reader will find a listing of anthologies of sophistic texts both in their original ancient Greek and in English translation. "The Sophists in General" contains sources that treat the sophists as a coherent group as well as some that problematize such treatments. In "Particular Sophists," citations deal exclusively (or at least primarily) with individual sophists (Antiphon, Critias, the anonymous *Dissoi Logoi,* Gorgias, Hippias, the anonymous Iamblichi, Prodicus, Protagoras, and Thrasymachus). "Neosophistic Rhetoric and Philosophy" includes a number of recent efforts to recover useful sophistic doctrines for contemporary rhetorical purposes. Finally, "Miscellaneous" lists sources of value to research on the sophists that were not easily placed within the other headings and categories that structure this bibliography.

Primary Sources

The untranslated Greek texts of the pre-Socratic philosophers and the sophists are found in:

Diels, Hermann, and Walther Kranz. *Die Fragmente Der Vorsokratiker.* 3 vols. Berlin: Wiedmann, 1951–52.

English translations of the sophistic texts in Diels and Kranz may be found in:

Freeman, Kathleen. *Ancilla to the Pre-Socratic Philosophers.* Cambridge: Harvard UP, 1948.

Sprague, Rosamond Kent, ed. *The Older Sophists.* Columbia: U of South Carolina P, 1972.

Of these translations, those in Sprague are the most cited in English-language scholarship.

The Sophists in General

The following sources treat the sophists as a relatively coherent group of teachers, with the exception of Kerferd's and Schiappa's works that problematize the notion of an identifiable sophistic epistemology, politics, or theory of rhetoric.

Barrett, Harold. *The Sophists: Rhetoric, Democracy, and Plato's Idea of Sophistry.* Novata, CA: Chandler and Sharp, 1987.

Bett, Richard. "The Sophists and Relativism." *Phronesis* 34 (1989): 139–69.

Bowersock, G. W. *Greek Sophists in the Roman Empire.* Oxford: Clarendon, 1969.

Brake, Robert J. "Pedants, Professors and the Law of the Excluded Middle: On Sophists and Sophistry." *Central States Speech Journal* 20 (1969): 122–29.

de Romilly, Jacqueline. *The Great Sophists in Periclean Athens.* Trans. Janet Lloyd. Oxford: Clarendon, 1992.

Dodds, E. R. "The Sophistic Movement and the Failure of Greek Liberalism." *The Ancient Concept of Progress and Other Essays on Greek Literature and Belief.* Ed. E. R. Dodds. Oxford: Clarendon, 1973. 92–105.

Enos, Richard Leo. *Greek Rhetoric Before Aristotle.* Prospect Heights, IL: Waveland, 1993.

Gibson, Walker. "In Praise of the Sophists." *College English* 55 (1993): 284–90.

Guthrie, W. K. C. *The Sophists.* Cambridge: Cambridge UP, 1971.

Hinks, D. A. G. "Tisias and Corax and the Invention of Rhetoric." *Classical Quarterly* 34 (1940): 61–69.

Hunt, Everett Lee. "On the Sophists." *The Province of Rhetoric.* Ed. Joseph Schwartz and John A. Rycenga. New York: Ronald, 1965. 69–84.

Jarratt, Susan. "The First Sophists and the Uses of History." *Rhetoric Review* 6 (1987): 67–77.

———. *Rereading the Sophists: Classical Rhetoric Refigured.* Carbondale: Southern Illinois UP, 1991.

———. "The Role of the Sophists in Histories of Consciousness." *Philosophy and Rhetoric* 23 (1990): 85–95.

Jarrett, James L. *The Educational Theory of the Sophists.* New York: Teachers College P, 1969.

Kerferd, G. B. "The First Greek Sophists." *Classical Review* os 64 (1950): 8–10.

———. *The Sophistic Movement.* Cambridge: Cambridge UP, 1981.

Lentz, Tony M. "Writing as Sophistry: From Preservation to Persuasion." *Quarterly Journal of Speech* 68 (1982): 60–68.

Levin, Saul. "The Origin of Grammar in Sophistry." *General Linguistics* 23 (1983): 41–47.

Poulakos, John. "Early Changes in Rhetorical Practice and Understanding: From the Sophists to Isocrates." *Texte* 8 (1989): 307–24.

———. "Rhetoric, the Sophists, and the Possible." *Communication Monographs* 51 (1984): 215–26.

———. *Sophistical Rhetoric in Classical Greece.* Columbia: U of South Carolina P, 1995.

———. "Terms for Sophistical Rhetoric." *Rethinking the History of Rhetoric.* Ed. Takis Poulakos. Boulder: Westview, 1993. 53–74.

———. "Toward a Sophistic Definition of Rhetoric." *Philosophy and Rhetoric* 16 (1983): 35–48.

Pullman, George L. "Reconsidering Sophistic Rhetoric in Light of Skeptical Epistemology." *Rhetoric Review* 13 (1994): 50–70.

Rapple, Brendan A. "The Early Greek Sophists: Creators of the Liberal Curriculum." *Journal of Thought* 28 (1993): 61–76.

Reimer, Milton K. "The Subjectivism of the Sophists: A Problem of Identity." *Journal of Thought* 13 (1978): 50–54.

Schiappa, Edward. "Sophistic Rhetoric: Oasis or Mirage." *Rhetoric Review* 10 (1991): 5–18.

Sesonske, Alexander. "To Make the Weaker Argument Defeat the Stronger." *Journal of the History of Philosophy* 6 (1968): 217–31.

Solmsen, Friedrich. *Intellectual Experiments of the Greek Enlightenment*. Princeton: Princeton UP, 1975.

Sutton, Jane. "The Marginalization of Sophistical Rhetoric and the Loss of History." *Rethinking the History of Rhetoric*. Ed. Takis Poulakos. Boulder: Westview, 1993. 75–90.

———. "Rereading Sophistical Arguments: A Political Intervention." *Argumentation* 5 (1991): 141–57.

Untersteiner, Mario. *The Sophists*. Trans. Kathleen Freeman. Oxford: Blackwell, 1954.

Wright, M. R. "Pre-Socratics and Sophists." *Phronesis* 40 (1995): 118–21.

Particular Sophists

Both Kerferd (in *The Sophistic Movement*) and Schiappa (in *Protagoras and Logos*) call for more extensive research on individual sophists that considers with greater scrutiny the historical situations that gave rise to the varied doctrines professed by these traveling teachers. In this section, I cite sources that examine the texts of individual sophists and resist generalizations about the sophists as a coherent group.

Antiphon

Antiphon the sophist, earliest of the ten great Attic orators, was born in Attica circa 480 BCE and specialized in the art of political rhetoric. An oligarch with ties to Sparta, he was instrumental in the overthrow of Athenian democracy in 411 BCE.

Avery, H. C. "One Antiphon or Two?" *Hermes* 90 (1982): 145–58.

Barnes, Jonathan. "New Light on Antiphon." *Polis* 7 (1987): 2–5.

Dodds, E. R. "The Nationality of Antiphon the Sophist." *Classical Review* ns 4 (1954): 94–95.

Dover, K. J. "The Chronology of Antiphon's Speeches." *Classical Quarterly* os 44 (1950): 44–60.

Due, B. *Antiphon: A Study in Argumentation*. Copenhagen: Museum Tusculanum, 1980.

Enos, Richard Leo. "Emerging Notions of Argument and Advocacy in Hellenic Litigation: Antiphon's *On the Murder of Herodes*." *Journal of the American Forensic Association* 16 (1980): 182–91.

Gagarin, Michael. "The Ancient Tradition on the Identity of Antiphon." *Greek, Roman, and Byzantine Studies* 31 (1990): 27–44.

———. *The Murder of Herodes: A Study of Antiphon 5*. New York: Lang, 1985.

———. "The Nature of Proofs in Antiphon." *Classical Philology* 85 (1990): 22–32.

Gagarin, Michael, and Douglas M. MacDowell, ed. and trans. *Antiphon and Andocides*. Austin: U of Texas P, 1998.

Innes, D. C. "Gorgias, Antiphon, and Sophistopolis." *Argumentation* 5 (1991): 221–31.

Jebb, Richard C. *The Attic Orators from Antiphon to Isaeus*. 2 vols. New York: Russell, 1962.

Lattimore, Steven. "Two Men in a Boat: Antiphon, *On the Murder of Herodes* 42." *Classical Quarterly* ns 37 (1987): 502–4.

Merlan, Philip. "Alexander the Great or Antiphon the Sophist?" *Classical Philology* 45 (1950): 161–66.

Morrison, J. S. "Socrates and Antiphon." *Classical Review* ns 5 (1955): 8–12.

———. "The *Truth* of Antiphon." *Phronesis* 8 (1963): 35–49.

Moulton, C. "Antiphon the Sophist and Democritus." *Museum Helveticum* 31 (1974): 129–39.

Nill, Michael. *Morality and Self-Interest in Protagoras, Antiphon, and Democritus*. Leiden, The Netherlands: Brill, 1985.

Reesor, Margaret E. "The *Truth* of Antiphon the Sophist." *Aperion* 20 (1987): 203–18.

Zuntz, G. "Once Again the Antiphontean Tetralogies." *Museum Helveticum* 6 (1949): 100–103.

Critias

One of Socrates's most successful students, Critias was an oligarchic tyrant (and associate of Antiphon) who led the Thirty in their bloody reign over Athens from 404 to 403 BCE.

Rosenmeyer, Thomas G. "The Family of Critias." *American Journal of Philology* 70 (1949): 404–10.

Stephans, Dorothy. *Critias: Life and Literary Remains*. Cincinnati, 1939.

Usher, S. "Xenophon, Critias, and Theramenes." *Journal of Hellenic Studies* 78 (1968): 128–35.

Wade-Gery, H. T. "Kritias and Herodes." *Classical Quarterly* os 39 (1945): 19–33.

Dissoi Logoi, Anonymous

The *Dissoi Logoi* (or *Dialexeis*) is an anonymous sophistic text written in the Protagorean tradition of opposing arguments.

Conley, Thomas M. "Dating the So-Called *Dissoi Logoi:* A Cautionary Note." *Ancient Philosophy* 5 (1985): 59–65.

Levi, Adolfo J. "On 'Twofold Statements.'" *American Journal of Philology* 61 (1940): 292–306.

Ramage, Edwin S. "An Early Trace of Socratic Dialogue." *American Journal of Philology* 82 (1961): 418–24.

Robinson, T. M. *Contrasting Arguments: An Edition of the* Dissoi Logoi. Salem, NH: Ayer, 1984.

———. "The *Dissoi Logoi* and Early Greek Scepticism." *Scepticism in the History of Philosophy: A Pan-American Dialogue.* Ed. Richard H. Popkin. Dordrecht, The Netherlands: Kluwer, 1996. 27–36.

———. "Matthew de Varis and the *Dissoi Logoi.*" *Classical Quarterly* ns 22 (1972): 195–98.

———. "A Sophist on Omniscience, Polymathy, and Omnicompetence: D. L. 8.1–13." *Illinois Classical Studies* 2 (1977): 125–35.

Roochnik, David. "Teaching Virtue: The Contrasting Arguments *(Dissoi Logoi)* of Antiquity." *Journal of Education* 179 (1997): 1–13.

Sprague, Rosamond Kent. "*Dissoi Logoi* or *Dialexeis:* Twofold Arguments." *Mind* 77 (1968): 155–67.

———. "A Platonic Parallel in the *Dissoi Logoi.*" *Journal of the History of Philosophy* 6 (1968): 160–61.

Taylor, A. E. "Socrates and the *Dissoi Logoi.*" *Varia Socratica.* Oxford: Oxford UP, 1911. 91–128.

Gorgias

Born in Leontini, Sicily, circa 480 BCE, Gorgias later moved to Athens to avoid persecution by Syracuse-backed oligarchs. Having lived most of his life writing and teaching in Athens, Gorgias upon his death was honored by its citizens with a gold statue in his likeness.

Brocker, W. "Gorgias Contra Parmenides." *Hermes* 86 (1958): 425–40.

Calogero, G. "Gorgias and the Socratic Principle *Nemo sua sponte peccat.*" *Journal of Hellenic Studies* 77 (1957): 12–17.

Consigny, Scott. "Gorgias's Use of the Epideictic." *Philosophy and Rhetoric* 25 (1992): 281–97.

———. "Sophistic Freedom: Gorgias and the Subversion of *Logos.*" *Pre/Text* 12 (1991): 225–35.

———. "The Style of Gorgias." *Rhetoric Society Quarterly* 22 (1992): 43–53.

Coulter, James A. "The Relation of the *Apology of Socrates* to Gorgias' *Defense of Palamedes* and Plato's Critique of Gorgianic Rhetoric." *Harvard Studies in Classical Philology* 68 (1964): 269–303.

Crowley, Sharon. "Of Gorgias and Grammatology." *College Composition and Communication* 30 (1979): 279–84.

Demand, Nancy. "Epicharmus and Gorgias." *American Journal of Philology* 92 (1971): 453–63.

Dodds, E. R. *Plato: Gorgias.* Oxford: Clarendon, 1959.

Duncan, Thomas S. "Gorgias' Theories of Art." *Classical Journal* 33 (1938): 402–15.

Engnell, Richard A. "Implications for Communication of the Rhetorical Epistemology of Gorgias of Leontini." *Western Journal of Speech Communication* 37 (1973): 175–84.

Enos, Richard Leo. "The Epistemology of Gorgias' Rhetoric: A Re-

Examination." *Southern Speech Communication Journal* 42 (1976): 35–51.

———. "Socrates Questions Gorgias: The Rhetorical Vector of Plato's 'Gorgias.'" *Argumentation* 5 (1991): 5–15.

———. "Why Gorgias of Leontini Traveled to Athens: A Study of Recent Epigraphical Evidence." *Rhetoric Review* 11 (1992): 1–15.

Gagarin, Michael. "On the Not-Being in Gorgias's *On Not-Being* (ONB)." *Philosophy and Rhetoric* 30 (1997): 38–40.

Gaines, Robert N. "Knowledge and Discourse in Gorgias's *On the Non-Existent or On Nature.*" *Philosophy and Rhetoric* 30 (1997): 1–12.

Garnons-Williams, B. H. "The Political Mission of Gorgias to Athens in 427 BC." *Classical Quarterly* os 25 (1931): 52–56.

Gronbeck, Bruce E. "Gorgias on Rhetoric and Poetic: A Rehabilitation." *Southern Speech Communication Journal* 38 (1972): 27–38.

Harrison, E. L. "Was Gorgias a Sophist?" *Phoenix* 18 (1964): 183–92.

Hays, Steve. "On the Skeptical Influence of Gorgias' *On Non-Being.*" *Journal of the History of Philosophy* 28 (1990): 327–37.

Hunter, V. "Thucydides, Gorgias, and Mass Psychology." *Hermes* 114 (1986): 412–29.

Innes, D. C. "Gorgias, Antiphon, and Sophistopolis." *Argumentation* 5 (1991): 221–31.

Jacoby, F. "The First Athenian Prose Writer." *Mnemosyne* 13 (1947): 13–64.

Kerferd, G. B. "Gorgias on Nature or That Which Is Not." *Phronesis* 1 (1955): 3–25.

Loenen, J. H. M. M. *Parmenides, Melissus, Gorgias: A Reinterpretation of Eleatic Philosophy.* Assen, The Netherlands: Van Gorcum, 1959.

MacDowell, Douglas. "Gorgias, Alkidamas, and the Cripps and Palatine Manuscripts." *Classical Quarterly* ns 11 (1961): 113–24.

Mackin, James A., Jr. *Gorgias: Encomium of Helen.* Bristol, UK: Bristol Classical Press, 1982.

Mansfeld, Jaap. "Historical and Philosophical Aspects of Gorgias' 'On What Is Not.'" *Siculorum Gymnasium* 38 (1985): 243–71.

McComiskey, Bruce. "Disassembling Plato's Critique of Rhetoric in the *Gorgias* (447a–466a)." *Rhetoric Review* 11 (1992): 79–90.

———. "Gorgias and the Art of Rhetoric: A Holistic Reading of the Extant Gorgianic Fragments." *Rhetoric Society Quarterly* 27 (1997): 5–24.

Mourelatos, Alexander P. D. "Gorgias on the Function of Language." *Siculorum Gymnasium* 38 (1985): 607–38.

Papillon, Terry L. "Isocrates on Gorgias and Helen: The Unity of the *Helen.*" *Classical Journal* 91 (1996): 377–91.

Porter, James I. "The Seductions of Gorgias." *Classical Antiquity* 12 (1993): 267–99.

Poulakos, John. "Gorgias' and Isocrates' Use of the Encomium." *Southern Communication Journal* 51 (1986): 300–307.

———. "Gorgias' *Encomium to Helen* and the Defense of Rhetoric." *Rhetorica* 1 (1983): 1–16.

———. "The Letter and the Spirit of the Text: Two Translations of Gorgias's *On Non-Being or On Nature*." *Philosophy and Rhetoric* 30 (1997): 41–44.

Poulakos, Takis. "The Historical Intervention of Gorgias' *Epitaphios:* A Brief History of Classical Funeral Orations." *Pre/Text* 10 (1989): 90–99.

Robinson, John M. "On Gorgias." *Exegesis and Argument.* Ed. E. N. Lee, A. P. D. Mourelatos, and R. M. Rorty. Assen, The Netherlands: Van Gorcum, 1973. 49–60.

Rosenmeyer, Thomas G. "Gorgias, Aeschylus, and *Apate.*" *American Journal of Philology* 76 (1955): 225–60.

Schiappa, Edward. "An Examination and Exculpation of the Composition Style of Gorgias of Leontini." *Pre/Text* 12 (1991): 237–57.

———. "Gorgias's *Helen* Revisited." *Quarterly Journal of Speech* 81 (1995): 310–24.

———. "Interpreting Gorgias's 'Being' in *On Not-Being or On Nature*." *Philosophy and Rhetoric* 30 (1997): 13–30.

Schiappa, Edward, and Stacey Hoffman. "Intertextual Argument in Gorgias's *On What Is Not:* A Formalization of Sextus, *Adv Math* 7.77–80." *Philosophy and Rhetoric* 27 (1994): 156–61.

Segal, Charles P. "Gorgias and the Psychology of the Logos." *Harvard Studies in Classical Philology* 66 (1962): 99–155.

Smith, Bromley. "Gorgias: A Study of Oratorical Style." *Quarterly Journal of Speech Education* 7 (1921): 335–59.

Solmsen, Friedrich. "Restoring an Antithesis to Gorgias (82 B 16 DK)." *Classical Quarterly* ns 37 (1987): 500–502.

Walters, Frank D. "Gorgias as Philosopher of Being: Epistemic Foundationalism in Sophistic Thought." *Philosophy and Rhetoric* 27 (1994): 143–55.

Hippias

Hippias of Ellis taught throughout Greece but mainly in Athens. He was famous for his excellent memory and his stylistic excesses.

Smith, Bromley. "Hippias and a Lost Canon of Rhetoric." *Quarterly Journal of Speech* 12 (1926): 129–45.

Iamblichi, Anonymous

This anonymous sophistic text quoted by Iamblichus was originally composed circa 400 BCE. It discusses politics, law, and virtue in the context of public life.

Cole, Andrew Thomas, Jr. "The Anonymous Iamblichi and Its Place in Greek Political Theory." *Harvard Studies in Classical Philology* 65 (1961): 127–63.

Prodicus

Prodicus of Ceos visited Athens frequently during the late-fifth and early-fourth centuries BCE. His chief rhetorical interest concerned accuracy in diction.

Biesecker, Susan L. "Rhetorical Discourse and the Constitution of the Subject: Prodicus' *The Choice of Heracles.*" *Argumentation* 5 (1991): 159–69.

Henrichs, Albert. "The Sophists and Hellenistic Religion: Prodicus as the Spiritual Father of the Isis Aretalogies." *Harvard Studies in Classical Philology* 88 (1984): 139–58.

Kerferd, G. B. "The 'Relativism' of Prodicus." *Bulletin of the John Rylands Library* 37 (1954): 249–56.

Smith, Bromley. "Prodicus of Ceos: The Sire of Synonymy." *Quarterly Journal of Speech Education* 6 (1920): 51–68.

Protagoras

Protagoras was born in Abdera circa 480 BCE, but he lived mostly in Athens throughout his life. Following pre-Socratic philosopher Heraclitus, Protagoras argued that there are opposing arguments regarding every issue.

Beattie, Paul. "Protagoras: The Maligned Philosopher." *Religious Humanism* 14 (1980): 108–15.

Bernsen, Niels O. "Protagoras' Homo-Mensura-Thesis." *Classica et Mediaevalia* 30 (1969): 109–44.

Burnyeat, M. F. "Protagoras and Self-Refutation in Later Greek Philosophy." *The Philosophical Review* 85 (1976): 44–69.

Burrell, P. S. "Man the Measure of All Things." *Philosophy* 7 (1932): 27–41, 168–84.

Chilton, C. W. "An Epicurean View of Protagoras." *Phronesis* 7 (1962): 105–9.

Cole, A. T. "The Apology of Protagoras." *Yale Classical Studies* 19 (1966): 101–18.

———. "The Relativism of Protagoras." *Yale Classical Studies* 22 (1972): 19–45.

Davison, J. A. "Protagoras, Democritus, and Anaxagoras." *Classical Quarterly* os 47 (1953): 33–45.

Donovan, Brian R. "The Project of Protagoras." *Rhetoric Society Quarterly* 23 (1993): 35–47.

Eldredge, Laurence. "Sophocles, Protagoras, and the Nature of Greek Culture." *Antioch Review* 25 (1965): 8–12.

Epps, P. H. "Protagoras' Famous Statement." *Classical Journal* 59 (1964): 223–26.

Frings, Manfred S. "Protagoras Rediscovered: Heidegger's Explication of Protagoras' Fragment." *Journal of Value Inquiry* 8 (1974): 112–23.

Gillespie, C. M. "The *Truth* of Protagoras." *Mind* 19 (1910): 470–92.

Glidden, David K. "Protagorean Obliquity." *History of Philosophy Quarterly* 5 (1988): 321–40.

———. "Protagorean Relativism and *Physis*." *Phronesis* 20 (1975): 209–27.

Jordan, James E. "Protagoras and Relativism: Criticisms Bad and Good." *Southwestern Journal of Philosophy* 2 (1971): 7–29.

Levi, Adolfo. "The Ethical and Social Thought of Protagoras." *Mind* 49 (1940): 284–302.

———. "Studies on Protagoras. The Man-Measure Principle: Its Meaning and Applications." *Philosophy* 40 (1940):147–67.

Loenen, Dirk. *Protagoras and the Greek Community.* Amsterdam: Noord-Holandsche, 1940.

McNeal, Richard A. "Protagoras the Historian." *History and Theory* 25 (1986): 299–318.

Mejer, Jorgen. "The Alleged New Fragment of Protagoras." *Hermes* 100 (1972): 175–78.

Morrison, J. S. "The Place of Protagoras in Athenian Public Life (460–415 BC)." *Classical Quarterly* 35 (1941): 1–16.

Moser, S., and G. L. Kustas. "A Comment on the 'Relativism' of Protagoras." *Phoenix* 20 (1966): 111–15.

Muir, J. V. "Protagoras and Education at Thourioi." *Greece and Rome* 29 (1982): 17–24.

Nill, Michael. *Morality and Self-Interest in Protagoras, Antiphon, and Democritus.* Leiden, The Netherlands: Brill, 1985.

Payne, David. "Rhetoric, Reality, and Knowledge: A Re-Examination of Protagoras' Concept of Rhetoric." *Rhetoric Society Quarterly* 16 (1986): 187–97.

Ritter, Michelle R. "In Search of the Real Protagoras." *Dialogue* 23 (1981): 58–65.

Roseman, N. "Protagoras and the Foundations of His Educational Thought." *Paedagogica Historica* 11 (1971): 75–89.

Schiappa, Edward. *Protagoras and Logos: A Study in Greek Philosophy and Rhetoric.* Columbia: U of South Carolina P, 1991.

Schiller, F. C. S. *Plato or Protagoras?* Oxford: Blackwell, 1908.

Sesonske, Alexander. "To Make the Weaker Argument Defeat the Stronger." *Journal of the History of Philosophy* 6 (1968): 217–31.

Simmons, George C. "The Humanism of the Sophists with Emphasis on Protagoras of Abdera." *Educational Theory* 19 (1969): 29–39.

———. "Protagoras on Education and Society." *Paedagogica Historica* 12 (1972): 518–37.

Smith, Bromley. "Protagoras of Abdera: The Father of Debate." *Quarterly Journal of Speech* 4 (1918): 196–215.

Stallknecht, Newton P. "Protagoras and the Critics." *Journal of Philosophy* 35 (1938): 39–45.

Versenyi, Laszlo. "Protagoras' Man-Measure Fragment." *American Journal of Philology* 83 (1962): 178–84.

Woodruff, Paul. "Didymus on Protagoras and the Protagoreans." *Journal of the History of Philosophy* 23 (1985): 483–97.

Zaslavsky, Robert. "The Platonic Godfather: A Note on the Protagoras Myth." *Journal of Value Inquiry* 16 (1982): 79–82.

Thrasymachus

Thrasymachus of Calcedon in Bithynia taught argumentative oratory and like Prodicus was also concerned with diction.

Astrene, Thomas. "An Analysis of Thrasymachus' True Definition of Rhetoric." *Dialogue* 20 (1978): 57–63.

Hagdopoulos, Demetrius. "Thrasymachus and Legalism." *Phronesis* 18 (1973): 204–8.

Harlap, Samuel. "Thrasymachus' Justice." *Political Theory* 7 (1979): 347–70.

Kerferd, G. B. "Thrasymachus and Justice: A Reply." *Phronesis* 9 (1964): 12–16.

Smith, Bromley. "Thrasymachus: A Pioneer Rhetorician." *Quarterly Journal of Speech* 13 (1927): 278–91.

White, Stephen A. "Thrasymachus the Diplomat." *Classical Philology* 90 (1995): 307–27.

Yunis, Harvey. "Thrasymachus B1: Discord, Not Diplomacy." *Classical Philology* 92 (1997): 58–66.

Neosophistic Rhetoric and Philosophy

The following sources examine the relationships between contemporary theories of rhetoric and sophistic doctrines. These authors appropriate sophistic doctrines for the purpose of solving problems in contemporary rhetorical theory, practice, and pedagogy.

Backman, Mark. *Rhetoric and the Rise of Self-Consciousness.* Woodbridge, CT: Ox Bow, 1991.

Ballif, Michelle. *Seduction, Sophistry, and the Woman with the Rhetorical Figure.* Carbondale: Southern Illinois UP, 2001.

Baumlin, James S. "Decorum, *Kairos,* and the 'New' Rhetoric." *Pre/Text* 5 (1984): 171–83.

Bertelsen, Dale A. "Sophistry, Epistemology, and the Media Context." *Philosophy and Rhetoric* 26 (1993): 296–301.

Biesecker, Susan L. "Rhetorical Discourse and the Constitution of the Subject: Prodicus' *The Choice of Heracles.*" *Argumentation* 5 (1991): 159–69.

Carter, Michael. "*Stasis* and *Kairos:* Principles of Social Construction in Classical Rhetoric." *Philosophy and Rhetoric* 7 (1988): 98–112.

Consigny, Scott. "Edward Schiappa's Reading of the Sophists." *Rhetoric Review* 14 (1996): 253–69.

———. "Gorgias's Use of the Epideictic." *Philosophy and Rhetoric* 25 (1992): 281–97.

Covino, William A. "Magic And/As Rhetoric." *Journal of Advanced Composition* 12 (1992): 349–58.

Crockett, Andy. "Gorgias's *Encomium of Helen:* Violent Rhetoric or Radical Feminism?" *Rhetoric Review* 13 (1994): 71–91.

Crowley, Sharon. "Of Gorgias and Grammatology." *College Composition and Communication* 30 (1979): 279–84.

———. "A Plea for the Revival of Sophistry." *Rhetoric Review* 7 (1989): 318–34.

Davis, D. Diane. *Breaking Up (at) Totality: A Rhetoric of Laughter.* Carbondale: Southern Illinois UP, 2000.

Frigerio, Carlo. "The Return of the Sophists." *South African Journal of Philosophy* 17 (1998): 275–300.

Hassett, Michael. "Sophisticated Burke: Kenneth Burke as a Neosophistic Rhetorician." *Rhetoric Review* 13 (1995): 371–90.

Hodges, Karen A. "Unfolding Sophistic and Humanistic Practice through *Ingenium.*" *Rhetoric Review* 15 (1996): 86–92.

Innes, D. C. "Gorgias, Antiphon, and Sophistopolis." *Argumentation* 5 (1991): 221–31.

Jarratt, Susan. "The First Sophists and Feminism: Discourses of the 'Other.'" *Hypatia* 5 (1990): 27–41.

———. "The First Sophists and the Politics of *Techne.*" *Discurrendo* 3 (1990): 2–7.

———. "The First Sophists and the Uses of History." *Rhetoric Review* 6 (1987): 67–77.

———. *Rereading the Sophists: Classical Rhetoric Refigured.* Carbondale: Southern Illinois UP, 1991.

———. "The Role of the Sophists in Histories of Consciousness." *Philosophy and Rhetoric* 23 (1990): 85–95.

———. "Toward a Sophistic Historiography." *Pre/Text* 8 (1987): 9–26.

Kinneavy, James L. *"Kairos:* A Neglected Concept in Classical Rhetoric." *Rhetoric and Praxis: The Contribution of Classical Rhetoric to Practical Reasoning.* Ed. Jean Dietz Moss. Washington, DC: Catholic U of America P, 1986. 79–105.

Kolb, David. *Postmodern Sophistications: Philosophy, Architecture, and Tradition.* Chicago: U of Chicago P, 1990.

Leff, Michael. "In Search of Ariadne's Thread: A Review of the Recent Literature on Rhetorical Theory." *Central States Speech Journal* 29 (1978): 73–91.

———. "Modern Sophistic and the Unity of Rhetoric." *The Rhetoric of the Human Sciences: Language and Argument in Scholarship and Public Affairs.* Ed. John S. Nelson, Allan Megill, and Donald N. McCloskey. Madison: U of Wisconsin P, 1987. 19–37.

Lentz, Tony M. "Writing as Sophistry: From Preservation to Persuasion." *Quarterly Journal of Speech* 68 (1982): 60–68.

Lindblom, Kenneth J. "Toward a Neosophistic Writing Pedagogy." *Rhetoric Review* 15 (1996): 93–109.

Mailloux, Steven, ed. *Rhetoric, Sophistry, Pragmatism.* New York: Cambridge UP, 1995.

McComiskey, Bruce. "Neo-Sophistic Rhetorical Theory: Sophistic Precedents for Contemporary Epistemic Rhetoric." *Rhetoric Society Quarterly* 24 (1994): 16–24.

Moss, Roger. "The Case for Sophistry." *Rhetoric Revalued.* Ed. Brian Vickers. Binghamton, NY: Center for Medieval and Early Renaissance Studies, 1982. 207–24.

Neel, Jasper. *Aristotle's Voice: Rhetoric, Theory, and Writing in America.* Carbondale: Southern Illinois UP, 1994.

———. "Dichotomy, Consubstantiality, Technical Writing, Literary Theory: The Double Orthodox Curse." *Journal of Advanced Composition* 12 (1992): 305–20.

———. *Plato, Derrida, and Writing.* Carbondale: Southern Illinois UP, 1988.

———. "Protagoras, Gorgias, Sophistry, and Democratic Departmental Governance." *ADE Bulletin* 90 (1988): 27–34.

Nelson, John S. "Political Theory as Political Rhetoric." *What Should Political Theory Be Now?* Ed. John S. Nelson. Albany: State U of New York P, 1983. 169–240.

Poulakos, John. "Gorgias' *Encomium to Helen* and the Defense of Rhetoric." *Rhetorica* 1 (1983): 1–16.

———. "Interpreting Sophistical Rhetoric: A Response to Schiappa." *Philosophy and Rhetoric* 23 (1990): 218–28.

———. "New Idioms for Sophistical Rhetoric: Introduction." *Argumentation* 5 (1991): 109–15.

———. "Rhetoric, the Sophists, and the Possible." *Communication Monographs* 51 (1984): 215–26.

———. "Terms for Sophistical Rhetoric." *Rethinking the History of Rhetoric.* Ed. Takis Poulakos. Boulder: Westview, 1993. 53–74.

———. "Toward a Sophistic Definition of Rhetoric." *Philosophy and Rhetoric* 16 (1983): 35–48.

Rapple, Brendan A. "The Early Greek Sophists: Creators of the Liberal Curriculum." *Journal of Thought* 28 (1993): 61–76.

Scenters-Zapico, John. "The Case for the Sophists." *Rhetoric Review* 11 (1993): 352–67.

Schiappa, Edward. "History and Neo-Sophistic Criticism: A Reply to Poulakos." *Philosophy and Rhetoric* 23 (1990): 307–15.

———. "Neo-Sophistic Rhetorical Criticism and the Historical Reconstruction of Sophistic Doctrines." *Philosophy and Rhetoric* 23 (1990): 192–217.

———. "Some of My Best Friends Are Neosophists: A Response to Consigny." *Rhetoric Review* 14 (1996): 272–79.

———. "Sophistic Rhetoric: Oasis or Mirage?" *Rhetoric Review* 10 (1991): 5–18.

Scott, J. Blake. "Sophistic Ethics in the Technical Writing Classroom: Teaching *Nomos,* Deliberation, and Action." *Technical Communication Quarterly* 4 (1995): 187–99.

Scott, Robert L. "On Viewing Rhetoric as Epistemic." *Central States Speech Journal* 18 (1967): 9–17.

Sheard, Cynthia Miecznikowski. "*Kairos* and Kenneth Burke's Psychology of Political and Social Communication." *College English* 55 (1993): 291–310.

Sullivan, Dale. "*Kairos* and the Rhetoric of Belief." *Quarterly Journal of Speech* 78 (1992): 317–32.

Sutton, Jane. "The Marginalization of Sophistical Rhetoric and the Loss of History." *Rethinking the History of Rhetoric*. Ed. Takis Poulakos. Boulder, CO: Westview, 1993. 75–90.

———. "Rereading Sophistical Arguments: A Political Intervention." *Argumentation* 5 (1991): 141–57.

Vitanza, Victor J. "Critical Sub/Versions of the History of Philosophical Rhetoric." *Rhetoric Review* 6 (1987): 41–66.

———. *Negation, Subjectivity, and the History of Rhetoric*. New York: State U of New York P, 1997.

———. "'Some More' Notes, Toward a 'Third' Sophistic." *Argumentation* 5 (1991): 117–39.

White, Eric Charles. *Kaironomia: On the Will-to-Invent*. Ithaca, NY: Cornell UP, 1987.

Wick, Audrey. "The Feminist Sophistic Enterprise: From Euripides to the Vietnam War." *Rhetoric Society Quarterly* 22 (1992): 27–38.

Miscellaneous

The following sources are of significant value to research on the sophists but are not easily categorized. Some, for example, deal with the sophists but move beyond the fifth century BCE in scope. Others examine particular issues, such as education, democracy, *apatê* (deception), and *kairos* (the opportune moment), that are crucial to an understanding of sophistic teachings but which do not relate to any sophist in particular or to the sophists as a group. Although these sources are, in a sense, marginalized under the heading "miscellaneous," they should not be neglected in research on sophistic doctrines.

Arthurs, Jeffrey. "The Term *Rhetor* in Fifth- and Fourth-Century BCE Greek Texts." *Rhetoric Society Quarterly* 23 (1994): 1–10.

Beck, Frederick A. G. *Greek Education: 450–350 BC*. New York: Barnes, 1964.

Belfiore, Elizabeth. "*Elenchus, Epode*, and Magic." *Phoenix* 34 (1980): 128–37.

Blank, David L. "Socratics Versus Sophists on Payment for Teaching." *Classical Antiquity* 4 (1985): 1–49.

Bryant, Donald C. *Ancient Greek and Roman Rhetoricians: A Biographical Dictionary.* Columbia, MO: Artcraft, 1968.

Buxton, R. G. A. *Persuasion in Greek Tragedy: A Study of Peitho.* Cambridge: Cambridge UP, 1982.

Clark, Donald. *Rhetoric in Greco-Roman Education.* New York: Columbia UP, 1957.

Classen, Carl Joachim. "The Study of Language Amongst Socrates' Contemporaries." *Sophistik.* Ed. Carl Joachim Classen. Darmstadt, Germany: Wissenschaft, 1976. 215–47.

Cole, A. Thomas. *The Origins of Greek Rhetoric.* Baltimore: Johns Hopkins UP, 1972.

———. "Who Was Corax?" *Illinois Classical Studies* 16 (1992): 65–84.

Connors, Robert J. "Greek Rhetoric and the Transition from Orality." *Philosophy and Rhetoric* 19 (1986): 38–65.

Consigny, Scott. "Nietzsche's Reading of the Sophists." *Rhetoric Review* 13 (1994): 5–29.

de Romilly, Jacqueline. *Magic and Rhetoric in Ancient Greece.* Cambridge: Harvard UP, 1974.

Dodds, E. R. *The Greeks and the Irrational.* Berkeley: U of California P, 1951.

Enos, Richard Leo. "Aristotle, Empedocles, and the Notion of Rhetoric." *In Search of Justice: The Indiana Tradition in Speech Communication.* Ed. R. Jensen and J. Hammerback. Amsterdam: Rodopi, 1987. 5–21.

Freeman, Kathleen. *Companion to the Pre-Socratic Philosophers.* 3rd ed. Oxford: Blackwell, 1953.

Gagarin, Michael, and Paul Woodruff, ed. *Early Greek Political Thought from Homer to the Sophists.* New York: Cambridge UP, 1995.

Gomperz, Theodor. *Greek Thinkers: A History of Ancient Philosophy.* Trans. Laurie Magnus. 4 vols. London: Murray, 1901.

Graeser, Andreas. "On Language, Thought, and Reality in Ancient Greek Philosophy." *Dialectica* 31 (1977): 359–88.

Gross, Nicholas. *Amatory Persuasion in Antiquity: Studies in Theory and Practice.* Newark: U of Delaware P, 1985.

Havelock, Eric A. *The Liberal Temper in Greek Politics.* New Haven: Yale UP, 1957.

———. "The Linguistic Task of the Pre-Socratics." *Language and Thought in Early Greek Philosophy.* Ed. Kevin Robb. La Salle, IL: Hegeler Institute, 1983. 7–82.

———. *The Literate Revolution in Greece and Its Cultural Consequences.* Princeton: Princeton UP, 1982.

———. *Preface to Plato.* Cambridge: Harvard UP, 1982.

Jacob, Bernard. "What If Aristotle Took Sophists Seriously? New Readings in Aristotle's *Rhetoric.*" *Rhetoric Review* 14 (1996): 237–52.

Jaeger, Werner. *Paideia: The Ideals of Greek Culture.* Rev. ed. 3 vols. Trans. Gilbert Highet. New York: Oxford UP, 1945.

Kennedy, George A. *The Art of Persuasion in Greece.* Princeton: Princeton UP, 1963.

———. *Classical Rhetoric and Its Christian and Secular Tradition from Ancient to Modern Times.* Chapel Hill: U of North Carolina P, 1980.

Lentz, Tony M. *Orality and Literacy in Hellenic Greece.* Carbondale: Southern Illinois UP, 1989.

Lloyd, G. E. R. *Polarity and Analogy: Two Types of Argumentation in Early Greek Thought.* Cambridge: Cambridge UP, 1966.

Loraux, Nicole. *The Invention of Athens: The Funeral Oration in the Classical City.* Cambridge: Harvard UP, 1986.

Moulder, James. "New Ideas on Early Greek Philosophy." *South African Journal of Philosophy* 2 (1983): 87–91.

Nehamas, Alexander. "Eristic, Antilogic, Sophistic, Dialectic: Plato's Demarcation of Philosophy from Sophistry." *History of Philosophy Quarterly* 7 (1990): 3–16.

Poster, Carol. "Being and Becoming: Rhetorical Ontology in Early Greek Thought." *Philosophy and Rhetoric* 29 (1996): 1–14.

Poulakos, John. "Hegel's Reception of the Sophists." *Western Journal of Speech Communication* 54 (1990): 160–71.

Poulakos, Takis. "Historiographies of the Tradition of Rhetoric: A Brief History of Classical Funeral Orations." *Western Journal of Speech Communication* 54 (1990): 172–88.

Rankin, H. D. *Sophists, Socratics, and Cynics.* New York: Barnes, 1983.

Robb, Kevin. *Literacy and Paideia in Ancient Greece.* New York: Oxford UP, 1994.

Rose, Peter W. "Sophocles' *Philoctetes* and the Teachings of the Sophists." *Harvard Studies in Classical Philology* 80 (1976): 49–105.

Schiappa, Edward. "Did Plato Coin *Rhêtorikê?*" *American Journal of Philology* 111 (1990): 457–70.

———. "*Rhêtorikê:* What's in a Name? Toward a Revised History of Early Greek Rhetorical Theory." *Quarterly Journal of Speech* 78 (1992): 1–15.

Shaw, Daniel C. "Nietzsche as Sophist: A Polemic." *International Philosophical Quarterly* 26 (1986): 331–39.

Solmsen, Friedrich. *Intellectual Experiments of the Greek Enlightenment.* Princeton: Princeton UP, 1975.

Stanton, G. R. "Sophists and Philosophers: Problems of Classification." *American Journal of Philology* 94 (1973): 350–64.

Swearingen, C. Jan. "Literate Rhetors and Their Illiterate Audiences: The Orality of Early Literacy." *Pre/Text* 7 (1986): 145–62.

Thom, Paul. "A Lesniewskian Reading of Ancient Ontology:

Parmenides to Democritus." *History and Philosophy of Logic* 7 (1986): 155–66.

Thomas, Rosalind. *Literacy and Orality in Ancient Greece.* New York: Cambridge UP, 1992.

Whitson, Steve. "On the Misadventures of the Sophists: Hegel's Tropological Appropriation of Rhetoric." *Argumentation* 5 (1991): 187–200.

Wiesenthal, Max. "Friedrich Nietzsche and the Greek Sophistic." Trans. Kerry K. Riley-Nuss. *Argumentation* 5 (1991): 201–20.

Wilcox, S. "The Scope of Early Rhetorical Instruction." *Harvard Studies in Classical Philology* 46 (1942): 121–55.

Wilkerson, K. E. "From Hero to Citizen: Persuasion in Early Greece." *Philosophy and Rhetoric* 15 (1982): 104–25.

Notes

Introduction

1. Scott Consigny, arguing against this distinction in Schiappa's scholarship, suggests that any historical interpretation is necessarily appropriative: "Neosophists are thoroughly 'historicist' in their accounts, for they insist that every historical account is itself an historically conditioned act of inventive writing and that every historian is inescapably situated in his or her own contingent historical perspective" ("Edward Schiappa's" 255). Although I agree with Consigny that all historical writing is interpretive, conditioned by the constraints and exigencies of the author's own historical moment (thus calling into question the rigid distinction between historical and rational reconstruction), nevertheless I also see no reason to confuse scholars whose purpose is to interpret historical doctrines with those scholars whose purpose is to appropriate these doctrines.

2. N. G. L. Hammond points out that Herodotus and Thucydides were creative authors who were in no way concerned with recording objective accounts of Greek history. "Taking for his field the span of human memory and the frontiers of the known world," Hammond argues, Herodotus

> composed his own "tales" or adapted the "tales" of his predecessors for particular areas, and he then imposed on the whole a unity, which derived not only from his own cast of mind but also from a central and dramatic theme, the conflict between West and East. (337)

Further, Hammond points out that in the absence of actual recorded words by the Greek heroes of the Persian Wars Thucydides wrote speeches that "contained not only the general sense of what was actually said, but also the arguments which [Thucydides] himself thought most appropriate to each occasion and speaker" (430).

1. Disassembling Plato's Critique of Rhetoric in the *Gorgias* (447a–466a)

1. For a more extended discussion of some of these same texts, see Maureen Taylor and Edward Schiappa's "How Accurate Is Plato's Portrayal of Gorgias of Leontini?"

2. Although I contrast democracy and oligarchy in this chapter (favoring the rule of the many), we must keep in mind that fifth-century BCE Athenian democracy was by no means an ideal government. In fact, under democratic rule, Athens permitted institutionalized slavery, and women were denied the possibility for citizenship and were not allowed to vote on public issues. However, given the brutality of the rulers in the oligarchic Athenian governments during the fifth century BCE, it is clear why democracy was the favored form of government for most Athenian citizens.

3. This law was not well received since the twenty-seven-year Peloponnesian War had engendered a respect for rhetorical skill among the democratic Athenian citizenry, and many of the sophists had come from democratic city-states to Athens specifically to teach the art of rhetoric to those who would enter politics and law. According to N. G. L. Hammond:

> When a democracy is at war, oratory becomes of greater importance, because more vital issues are debated and more stirring leadership is demanded. This was doubly so at Athens. For the people at mass meetings not only decided policy but also tried all magistrates, so that a politician without oratory lacked the means of carrying conviction and of escaping condemnation. Cimon and Pericles, both great orators, had been trained in the school of family tradition, but at the beginning of the war oratory was becoming a marketable art which could be sold to many would-be politicians or advocates. . . . In the democratic states of Sicily, Corax started the study of oratory as a technique, and Tisias and Gorgias were already famous exponents of this technique when they visited Athens in 427 as members of an embassy from Leontini. Their eloquence amazed the Athenian people, . . . and Gorgias won a Panhellenic reputation by delivering prize speeches at Delphi and Olympia. (420)

4. *Epistêmê* is knowledge already acquired, and *mathêsis* is the process by which knowledge is acquired. *Pistis* is the state of belief or agreement resulting from successful persuasion, and *doxa* is the opinion upon which judgments are based. Both *pistis* and *doxa* can be translated "opinion" but in *pistis* that opinion is the result of persuasion and in *doxa* it is the catalyst of judgment.

5. Throughout this chapter, when I refer to "Gorgias the sophist," I mean the historical figure, and when I refer to "Plato's Gorgias," I mean the dialogic character.

6. This and all subsequent translations of Gorgias's extant texts are my own based on the texts in Hermann Diels and Walther Kranz's *Die Fragmente Der Vorsokratiker.*

2. Gorgias and the Art of Rhetoric

1. Most translations of the *Helen* render *eros* as "love"; however, it is clear that in this passage Gorgias refers only to external beauty as the object of desire. Love has little to do with Helen's abduction, since the flow of *eros* in that case would be mutually and willingly exchanged rather than imposed from outside and beyond Helen's capacity to resist it.

2. My purpose in comparing Aristotle's *topoi* in the *Rhetoric* to Gorgias's *topoi* in the *Palamedes* is twofold: first, to suggest that Gorgias's fifth-century BCE text contains some of the same "technical" characteristics of later rhetorical treatises and should thus be considered part of a rhetorical *technê;* and second, to suggest that Aristotle's discussion of rhetorical invention was probably not news to his ancient audiences. Too often we ascribe to Aristotle an originary function when he is in fact summarizing rhetorical strategies that had existed for centuries.

3. Ethical appeals, in the context of fifth-century BCE Athenian public life, were certainly critical for rhetorical success. As J. K. Davies points out in *Democracy and Classical Greece:*

> No public man, however honest, could avoid using the available [rhetorical] techniques and consciously creating a *persona* for himself, reflected above all in the style and presentation of his public utterances: and no member of the Assembly or jury, however stupid, could avoid having to make repeated choices among competing *personae*. (126)

According to Cole, the absence of ethical considerations characterizes the "a-technical," "proto-rhetorical" texts of the sophistic movement (73, 79); however, *ethos* is an undeniably prominent theme throughout the *Palamedes*.

3. Neosophistic Rhetorical Theory

1. It is important to note here that, while I accept the spirit of Jarratt's argument, she is, nevertheless, one of the most relentless essentialists in neosophistic scholarship. In fact, Jarratt sets up her view of sophistic historiography with the claim that "the sophists translated the natural scientists' observations about the temporality of human existence into a coherent body of commentary on the use of discourse in the function of the social order" (263–64). Of course, a glance through Kathleen Freeman's *Ancilla to the Pre-Socratic Philosophers* reveals that not all natural scientists believed in the temporality of human existence, and a glance through Rosamond Kent Sprague's *The Older Sophists* reveals that sophistic doctrines do not comprise a coherent body of commentary on anything, and only some of them were directly concerned with the art of *logos* (or what Jarratt calls "discourse").

2. Edward Schiappa, however, argues that the sophists packed too lightly for the trip, and some of their bags were confiscated in customs; further, many of the sophists simply missed the flight. As a result, Schiappa suggests, "We do not need the fiction of 'sophistic rhetoric' as a way into pressing contemporary issues. In a culture saturated by rhetoric, we need not seek refuge in a romanticized fictionalization of a place 'long ago and far away'" ("Sophistic" 14). Sophistic rhetoric, in other words, loses strength in a modern context, and as such it is not an asset but a liability for articulations of modern rhetoric. Nevertheless, many of the sophists have traveled, have made the long and difficult journey, and quite a number of their bags have made it through. They are here with us, looking over our shoulders as we write. The sophists have had profound influences on some of the most important developments in rhetorical

theory and composition studies, and to neglect their journey into the twentieth century and beyond would be first, to neglect a critical aspect of rhetoric's history and second, to neglect one of the richest historical resources.

5. The Global Village, Multiculturalism, and the Functions of Sophistic Rhetoric

1. Communities are "imagined," Anderson argues, "because the members of even the smallest nation will never know most of their fellow-members, meet them, or even hear of them, yet in the minds of each lives the image of their communion" (6).

Works Cited

Adorno, Theodor W. "The Culture Industry Reconsidered." Trans. Anson G. Rabinbach. *Critical Theory and Society: A Reader.* Ed. Stephen Eric Bronner and Douglas MacKay Kellner. New York: Routledge, 1989. 128–35.

Aeschylus. *Prometheus Bound.* Trans. David Green. *Greek Tragedies.* Ed. David Green and Richard Lattimore. Chicago: U of Chicago P, 1960. 61–105.

Anderson, Benedict. *Imagined Communities: Reflections on the Origin and Spread of Nationalism.* London: Verso, 1991.

Ang, Ien. "In the Realm of Uncertainty: The Global Village and Capitalist Postmodernity." *Communication Theory Today.* Ed. David Crowley and David Mitchell. Stanford, CA: Stanford UP, 1994. 193–213.

Aristides. *Orations* (46). Trans. William O'Neil. "Name and Notion." *The Older Sophists.* Ed. Rosamond Kent Sprague. Columbia: U of South Carolina P, 1972. 1.

Aristotle. *On Rhetoric: A Theory of Civic Discourse.* Trans. George A. Kennedy. New York: Oxford UP, 1991.

———. *Sophistical Refutations.* Trans. W. A. Pickard-Cambridge. *The Complete Works of Aristotle.* Ed Jonathan Barnes. Vol. 1. Princeton: Princeton UP, 1984. 278–314.

Barilli, Renato. *Rhetoric.* Trans. Giuliana Menozzi. Minneapolis: U of Minnesota P, 1989.

Barnlund, Dean C. *Public and Private Self in Japan and the United States.* Tokyo: Simul, 1975.

Baudrillard, Jean. *Seduction.* Trans. Brian Singer. New York: St. Martin's, 1990.

———. *Simulations.* Trans. Paul Foss, Paul Patton, and Philip Beitchman. New York: Semiotext(e), 1983.

Baumlin, James S. "Decorum, *Kairos,* and the 'New' Rhetoric." *Pre/Text* 5 (1984): 171–83.

Benjamin, Walter. "Theses on the Philosophy of History." *Critical Theory and Society: A Reader.* Ed. Stephen Eric Bronner and Douglas MacKay Kellner. New York: Routledge, 1989. 255–63.

Berlin, James A. "Aristotle's Rhetoric in Context: Interpreting Historically." *A Rhetoric of Doing: Essays on Written Discourse in Honor of James L. Kinneavy.* Ed. Stephen P. Witte, Neil Nakadate, and Roger Cherry. Carbondale: Southern Illinois UP, 1992. 55–64.

———. *Rhetorics, Poetics, and Cultures: Refiguring College English Studies.* Urbana, IL: NCTE, 1996.

Bialostosky, Don H. "Antilogics, Dialogics, and Sophistic Social Psychology: Michael Billig's Reinvention of Bakhtin from Protagorean Rhetoric." *Rhetoric, Sophistry, Pragmatism*. Ed. Steven Mailloux. New York: Cambridge UP, 1995. 82–93.

Burke, Kenneth. "Terministic Screens." *Language as Symbolic Action: Essays on Life, Literature, and Method*. Berkeley: U of California P, 1966. 44–62.

———. "What Are the Signs of What? (A Theory of 'Entitlement')." *Language as Symbolic Action: Essays on Life, Literature, and Method*. Berkeley: U of California P, 1966. 359–79.

Burnet, John. *Greek Philosophy: From Thales to Plato*. New York: Macmillan, 1968.

Buxton, R. G. A. *Persuasion in Greek Tragedy: A Study of Peitho*. Cambridge: Cambridge UP, 1982.

Chase, J. Richard. "The Classical Conception of Epideictic." *Quarterly Journal of Speech* 47 (1961): 293–300.

Clark, Donald. *Rhetoric in Greco-Roman Education*. New York: Columbia UP, 1957.

Cole, Thomas. *The Origins of Rhetoric in Ancient Greece*. Baltimore: Johns Hopkins UP, 1991.

Consigny, Scott. "Edward Schiappa's Reading of the Sophists." *Rhetoric Review* 14 (1996): 253–69.

———. "Gorgias's Use of the Epideictic." *Philosophy and Rhetoric* 25 (1992): 281–97.

———. "Sophistic Challenges: Gorgias' Epideictic Rhetoric and Postmodern Performance Art." *Rhetoric in the Vortex of Cultural Studies*. Ed. Arthur Walzer. St. Paul, MN: Rhetoric Society of America, 1992. 110–19.

Covino, William A. "Magic And/As Rhetoric." *Journal of Advanced Composition* 12 (1992): 349–58.

Crowley, Sharon. "Of Gorgias and Grammatology." *College Composition and Communication* 30 (1979): 279–84.

———. "A Plea for the Revival of Sophistry." *Rhetoric Review* 7 (1989): 318–34.

Crowley, Sharon, and Debra Hawhee. *Ancient Rhetorics for Contemporary Students*. 2nd ed. Boston: Allyn, 1999.

Cruz, Jon. "From Farce to Tragedy: Reflections on the Reification of Race at Century's End." *Mapping Multiculturalism*. Ed. Avery F. Gordon and Christopher Newfield. Minneapolis: U of Minnesota P, 1996. 19–39.

Davies, J. K. *Democracy and Classical Greece*. Stanford: Stanford UP, 1983.

de Certeau, Michel. *The Practice of Everyday Life*. Trans. Steven Rendall. Berkeley: U of California P, 1984.

———. *The Writing of History*. Trans. Tom Conley. New York: Columbia UP, 1988.

de Romilly, Jacqueline. *The Great Sophists in Periclean Athens*. Trans. Janet Lloyd. Oxford: Clarendon, 1992.

Derrida, Jacques. "Sending: On Representation." Trans. Peter Caws and Mary Ann Caws. *Social Research* 49 (1982): 294–326.

———. "Signature Event Context." *Margins of Philosophy*. Trans. Alan Bass. Chicago: U of Chicago P, 1982. 307–30.

——. *Speech and Phenomena*. Trans. David B. Allison. Evanston, IL: Northwestern UP, 1973.

——. "Structure, Sign, and Play in the Discourse of the Human Sciences." *Writing and Difference*. Trans. Alan Bass. Chicago: U of Chicago P, 1978. 278–93.

——. "The Theater of Cruelty and the Closure of Representation." *Writing and Difference*. Trans. Alan Bass. Chicago: U of Chicago P, 1978. 232–49.

Diels, Hermann, and Walther Kranz. *Die Fragmente Der Vorsokratiker*. 3 vols. Berlin: Weidmann, 1951–52.

DiStephano, Joseph J. "Case Methods in International Management Training." *Handbook of Intercultural Communication*. Ed. Molefi Kete Asante, Eileen Newmark, and Cecil A. Blake. London: Sage, 1979. 421–46.

Dodds, E. R. *The Greeks and the Irrational*. Berkeley: U of California P, 1951.

——. Introduction. *Plato: Gorgias*. Oxford: Clarendon, 1959. 1–66.

Ducrey, Pierre. *Warfare in Ancient Greece*. Trans. Janet Lloyd. New York: Schocken, 1985.

Enos, Richard Leo. "Why Gorgias of Leontini Traveled to Athens: A Study of Recent Epigraphical Evidence." *Rhetoric Review* 11 (1992): 1–15.

Field, G. C. Introduction. *Plato: Socratic Dialogues*. By W. D. Woodhead. London: Nelson, 1962. i–xxi.

Foucault, Michel. *The Order of Things: An Archaeology of the Human Sciences*. New York: Vintage, 1973.

Freeman, Kathleen. *Ancilla to the Pre-Socratic Philosophers*. Cambridge: Harvard UP, 1948.

——. *The Pre-Socratic Philosophers: A Companion to Diels, Die Fragmente Der Vorsokratiker*. 3rd ed. Oxford: Basil Blackwell, 1953.

Gibson, Walker. "In Praise of the Sophists." *College English* 55 (1993): 284–90.

Giroux, Henry. *Border Crossings: Cultural Workers and the Politics of Education*. New York: Routledge, 1992.

——. *Pedagogy and the Politics of Hope: Theory, Culture, and Schooling*. Boulder, CO: Westview, 1997.

Golding, Peter. "Global Village or Global Pillage?" *Capitalism and the Information Age: The Political Economy of the Global Communication Revolution*. Ed. Robert W. McChesney, Ellen Meiksins Wood, and John Bellamy Foster. New York: Monthly Review, 1998. 69–86.

Gramsci, Antonio. *Selections from the Prison Notebooks*. Ed. and trans. Q. Hoare and G. Nowell-Smith. London: Lawrence, 1974.

Greenblatt, Stephen J. *Learning to Curse*. New York: Routledge, 1990.

Gross, Nicholas. *Amatory Persuasion in Antiquity: Studies in Theory and Practice*. Newark: U of Delaware P, 1985.

Guthrie, W. K. C. *The Sophists*. Cambridge: Cambridge UP, 1971.

Hall, Edward T., and Mildred Reed Hall. *Understanding Cultural Differences*. Yarmouth, ME: Intercultural, 1990.

Hall, Stuart. "Encoding/Decoding." *Culture, Media, Language*. London: Hutchinson, 1980. 128–38.

Hammond, N. G. L. *A History of Greece to 322 BC*. 3rd ed. Oxford: Clarendon, 1986.

Havelock, Eric A. "The Linguistic Task of the Presocratics." *Language and Thought in Early Greek Philosophy*. Ed. Kevin Robb. La Salle, IL: Hegeler Institute, 1983. 7–82.

Hays, Steve. "On the Skeptical Influence of Gorgias' *On Non-Being*." *Journal of the History of Philosophy* 28 (1990): 327–37.

Hesiod. *Works and Days*. In *The Homeric Hymns and Homerica*. Trans. Hugh G. Evelyn White. Cambridge: Harvard UP, 1936. 2–65.

Homer. *The Iliad*. Trans. A. T. Murray. 2 vols. Cambridge: Harvard UP, 1957.

Hurst, Paul, and Grahame Thompson. *Globalization in Question: The International Economy and the Possibilities of Governance*. Cambridge: Polity, 1996.

Irwin, Terence. Introduction. *Plato's Gorgias*. Oxford: Clarendon, 1979. 1–12.

Jameson, Fredric. "Periodizing the '60s." *The '60s Without Apology*. Ed. Sohnya Sayres et al. Minneapolis: U of Minnesota P, 1984. 178–209.

Jarratt, Susan. *Rereading the Sophists: Classical Rhetoric Refigured*. Carbondale: Southern Illinois UP, 1991.

———. "Speaking to the Past: Feminist Historiography in Rhetoric. *PrelText* 11 (1990): 189–209.

———. "Toward a Sophistic Historiography." *PrelText* 8 (1987): 9–26.

Kennedy, George A., trans. *Aristotle, On Rhetoric: A Theory of Civic Discourse*. New York: Oxford UP, 1991.

Kerferd, G. B. *The Sophistic Movement*. Cambridge: Cambridge UP, 1981.

Kinneavy, James L. "*Kairos*: A Neglected Concept in Classical Rhetoric." *Rhetoric and Praxis: The Contribution of Classical Rhetoric to Practical Reasoning*. Ed. Jean Dietz Moss. Washington, DC: Catholic U of America P, 1986. 79–105.

Krentz, Peter. *The Thirty at Athens*. Ithaca, NY: Cornell UP, 1982.

Lanham, Richard A. *Literacy and the Survival of Humanism*. New Haven: Yale UP, 1983.

Leff, Michael C. "In Search of Ariadne's Thread: A Review of the Recent Literature on Rhetorical Theory." *Central States Speech Journal* 29 (1978): 73–91.

———. "Modern Sophistic and the Unity of Rhetoric." *The Rhetoric of the Human Sciences: Language and Argument in Scholarship and Public Affairs*. Ed. John S. Nelson, Allan Megill, and Donald N. McCloskey. Madison: U of Wisconsin P, 1987. 19–37.

Lentz, Tony M. *Orality and Literacy in Hellenic Greece*. Carbondale: Southern Illinois UP, 1989.

Lloyd, G. E. R. *The Revolutions of Wisdom: Studies in the Claims and Practice of Ancient Greek Science*. Berkeley: U of California P, 1987.

Lodge, David. "Jacques Derrida." *Modern Criticism and Theory: A Reader*. Ed. David Lodge. London: Longman, 1988. 107–8.

Lyotard, Jean-François. "Beyond Representation." Trans. Jonathan Culler. *The Lyotard Reader*. Ed. Andrew Benjamin. Cambridge MA: Blackwell, 1989. 155–68.

———. *The Differend: Phrases in Dispute*. Trans. Georges Van Den Abbeele. Minneapolis: U of Minnesota P, 1988.

———. *Heidegger and "the jews."* Trans. Andreas Michel and Mark Roberts. Minneapolis: U of Minnesota P, 1990.

Mailloux, Steven. "Introduction: Sophistry and Rhetorical Pragmatism." *Rhetoric, Sophistry, Pragmatism.* Ed. Steven Mailloux. New York: Cambridge UP, 1995. 1–31.

McChesney, Robert W. "The Political Economy of Global Communication." *Capitalism and the Information Age: The Political Economy of the Global Communication Revolution.* Ed. Robert W. McChesney, Ellen Meiksins Wood, and John Bellamy Foster. New York: Monthly Review, 1998. 1–26.

McLaren, Peter. "White Terror and Oppositional Agency: Towards a Critical Multiculturalism." *Multicultural Education, Critical Pedagogy, and the Politics of Difference.* Ed. Christine E. Sleeter and Peter McLaren. New York: State U of New York P, 1995. 33–70.

McLuhan, Marshal, and Bruce Powers. *The Global Village: Transformations in World Life and Media in the Twenty-First Century.* New York: Oxford UP, 1989.

Morley, David, and Kevin Robins. *Spaces of Identity: Global Media, Electronic Landscapes, and Cultural Boundaries.* London: Routledge, 1995.

Moss, Roger. "The Case for Sophistry." *Rhetoric Revalued.* Ed. Brian Vickers. Binghamton, NY: Center for Medieval and Early Renaissance Studies, 1982. 207–24.

Nazer, Hisham M. *Power of a Third Kind: The Western Attempt to Colonize the Global Village.* London: Praeger, 1999.

Neel, Jasper. *Plato, Derrida, and Writing.* Carbondale: Southern Illinois UP, 1988.

Nolan, Riall W. *Communicating and Adapting Across Cultures: Living and Working in the Global Village.* London: Bergin, 1999.

Plato. *Gorgias.* Trans. W. D. Woodhead. *Plato: The Collected Dialogues.* Ed. Edith Hamilton and Huntington Cairns. Princeton, NJ: Princeton UP, 1961. 229–307.

———. *Meno.* Trans. W. K. C. Guthrie. *Plato: The Collected Dialogues.* Ed. Edith Hamilton and Huntington Cairns. Princeton, NJ: Princeton UP, 1961. 353–84.

———. *Phaedrus.* Trans. R. Hackforth. *Plato: The Collected Dialogues.* Ed. Edith Hamilton and Huntington Cairns. Princeton, NJ: Princeton UP, 1961. 475–525.

———. *Protagoras.* Trans. W. K. C. Guthrie. *Plato: The Collected Dialogues.* Ed. Edith Hamilton and Huntington Cairns. Princeton, NJ: Princeton UP, 1961. 308–52.

———. *Republic.* Trans. Paul Shorey. *Plato: The Collected Dialogues.* Ed. Edith Hamilton and Huntington Cairns. Princeton, NJ: Princeton UP, 1961. 575–844.

———. *Sophist.* Trans. F. M. Cornford. *Plato: The Collected Dialogues.* Ed. Edith Hamilton and Huntington Cairns. Princeton, NJ: Princeton UP, 1961. 957–1017.

———. *Timaeus.* Trans. Benjamin Jowett. *Plato: The Collected Dialogues.* Ed. Edith Hamilton and Huntington Cairns. Princeton, NJ: Princeton UP, 1961. 1151–211.

Popper, Karl. *The Poverty of Historicism.* Boston: Beacon, 1957.

Poulakos, John. *Sophistical Rhetoric in Classical Greece.* Columbia: U of South Carolina P, 1995.

———. "Toward a Sophistic Definition of Rhetoric." *Philosophy and Rhetoric* 16 (1983): 35–48.

Poulakos, Takis. "The Historical Intervention of Gorgias' *Epitaphios:* The Genre of Funeral Oration and the Athenian Institution of Public Burials." *Pre/Text* 10 (1989): 90–99.

———. "Towards a Cultural Understanding of Classical Epideictic Oratory." *Pre/Text* 9 (1988): 147–66.

Pratt, Mary Louise. "Arts of the Contact Zone." *Profession 91.* New York: MLA, 1991. 33–40.

Robinson, T. M. *Contrasting Arguments: An Edition of the* Dissoi Logoi. Salem, NH: Ayer, 1984.

Rosenmeyer, Thomas G. "Gorgias, Aeschylus, and *Apate.*" *American Journal of Philology* 76 (1955): 225–60.

Royer, Daniel J. "New Challenges to Epistemic Rhetoric." *Rhetoric Review* 9 (1991): 282–97.

Said, Edward. "Traveling Theory." *The World, the Text, and the Critic.* Cambridge: Harvard UP, 1983. 226–47.

Schiappa, Edward. "Isocrates' *Philosophia* and Contemporary Pragmatism." *Rhetoric, Sophistry, Pragmatism.* Ed. Steven Mailloux. New York: Cambridge UP, 1995. 33–60.

———. "Neo-Sophistic Rhetorical Criticism or the Historical Reconstruction of Sophistic Doctrines?" *Philosophy and Rhetoric* 23 (1990): 192–217.

———. *Protagoras and Logos: A Study in Greek Philosophy and Rhetoric.* Columbia: U of South Carolina P, 1991.

———. "*Rhêtorikê:* What's in a Name? Toward a Revised History of Early Greek Rhetorical Theory." *Quarterly Journal of Speech* 78 (1992): 1–15.

———. "Sophistic Rhetoric: Oasis or Mirage?" *Rhetoric Review* 10 (1991): 5–18.

Schnapper, Melvin. "Multinational Training for Multinational Corporations." *Handbook of Intercultural Communication.* Ed. Molefi Kete Asante, Eileen Newmark, and Cecil A. Blake. London: Sage, 1979. 447–74.

Scott, Robert L. "On Viewing Rhetoric as Epistemic." *Central States Speech Journal* 18 (1967): 9–17.

Segal, Charles P. "Gorgias and the Psychology of the Logos." *Harvard Studies in Classical Philology* 66 (1962): 99–155.

Sprague, Rosamond Kent, ed. *The Older Sophists.* Columbia: U of South Carolina P, 1972.

Stanford, W. B. *Greek Tragedy and the Emotions.* Boston: Routledge, 1983.

Taylor, Maureen, and Edward Schiappa. "How Accurate is Plato's Portrayal of Gorgias of Leontini?" *Rhetoric in the Vortex of Cultural Studies.* Ed. Arthur Walzer. Minneapolis: Rhetoric Society, 1993. 23–31.

Thompson, W. H. Introduction. *The Gorgias of Plato.* New York: Arno, 1973. i–xx.

Thucydides. *The Peloponnesian War*. Trans. Benjamin Jowett. Vol. 1 of *The Greek Historians: The Complete and Unabridged Historical Works of Herodotus, Thucydides, Xenophon, and Arrian*. Ed. Francis R. B. Godolphin. 2 vols. New York: Random House, 1942. 567–1001.

Tomlinson, John. *Cultural Imperialism*. Baltimore: Johns Hopkins UP, 1991.

Trimbur, John. "Taking the Social Turn: Teaching Writing Post-Process." *College Composition and Communication* 45 (1994): 108–18.

Untersteiner, Mario. *The Sophists*. Trans. Kathleen Freeman. Oxford: Blackwell, 1954.

Vakhrushev, Vasily. *Neocolonialism: Methods and Manoeuvers*. Trans. Katherine Judelson. Moscow: Progress, 1973.

Vitanza, Victor J. *Negation, Subjectivity, and the History of Rhetoric*. New York: State U of New York P, 1997.

———. "'Some More' Notes, Toward a 'Third' Sophistic." *Argumentation* 5 (1991): 117–39.

White, Eric Charles. *Kaironomia: On the Will-to-Invent*. Ithaca, NY: Cornell UP, 1987.

Wick, Audrey. "The Feminist Sophistic Enterprise: From Euripides to the Vietnam War." *Rhetoric Society Quarterly* 22 (1992): 27–38.

Williams, Raymond. *Marxism and Literature*. Oxford: Oxford UP, 1977.

Willis, Paul. "Notes on Method." *Culture, Media, Language*. London: Hutchinson, 1980. 89–95.

Xenophon. *Hellenica*. Trans. Henry G. Dakyns. Vol. 2 of *The Greek Historians: The Complete and Unabridged Historical Works of Herodotus, Thucydides, Xenophon, and Arrian*. Ed. Francis R. B. Godolphin. 2 vols. New York: Random House, 1942. 3–221.

———. *Memorabilia* (1.2.12–31). Trans. Donald Norman Levin. "Critias." *The Older Sophists*. Ed. Rosamond Kent Sprague. Columbia: U of South Carolina P, 1972. 244–45.

Index

Adorno, Theodor W., 92, 117
Aeschylean Dialogues, 43
Aeschylus, 40–41; *Prometheus Bound,*
  40–41
Affirmative Deconstruction. *See* De-
  construction, Affirmative
Aitiai, 21
Alcibiades, 19–20
Alêtheia (Alêtheian, Alêtheias), 24, 27,
  38, 44, 47, 49, 51, 52. *See also*
  Truth
Alexander, 41–42
Alogon, 21
Anankê, 28, 47, 113
Anaxarchus, 111–12
Anderson, Benedict, 100, 142
Ang, Ien, 100, 105–8
Anthrôpinêi Promêthiai, 39–41. *See*
  also Promêthiai
Antiphon, 6, 124–25
Antistrophos, 33
Anytus, 2
Apatê, 52, 134
Apollo, 43
Aretê, 49
Aristides, 3, 6
Aristos, 42
Aristotle, 1, 2, 3, 33, 34, 47–52, 61,
  63, 90–91, 92, 141; *Nichomochean
  Ethics,* 51–52; *Rhetoric,* 3, 33, 47–
  48, 49, 50–51, 52, 90–91, 141; *So-
  phistical Refutations,* 2–3
Aronowitz, Stanley, 74
Atechnê, 52
Athens, 3, 6, 13, 19, 20, 33, 37, 74,

76, 110, 111, 125, 126, 128, 129,
  140

Bacon, Francis, 63
Bakhtin, Mikhail, 71–72
Barilli, Renato, 17
Barnlund, Dean C., 100, 101
Baudrillard, Jean, 77, 80, 83–85, 86,
  88. *See also* Seduction; Simulation
Baumlin, James, S. 62, 63–64
Beltistos, 21
Benjamin, Walter, 5
Berlin, James A., 62, 91, 97
Bia, 39, 41
Bialostosky, Don H., 71–72
Burke, Kenneth, 61, 77, 79, 80–82, 88
Burnet, John, 18
Buxton, R. G. A., 39

Capitalism, 101, 113–14; Centrifugal,
  114; Global, 101; Late, 113
Cassirer, Ernst, 59
Centrifugal Capitalism. *See* Capital-
  ism, Centrifugal
Chase, Richard J., 91
Cicero, 63
Cimon, 140
Clark, Donald, 18
Cole, Thomas, 38, 141
Communication, 5, 28, 60, 68, 82–83,
  85–88, 89, 97–108, 110, 116; In-
  tercultural, 99, 100, 101, 110
Composition, 11, 57, 58, 64–68, 70–
  71, 74, 77, 142
Consigny, Scott, 92–93, 139

151

Bruce McComiskey, a Kinneavy Award-winning scholar and author of *Teaching Composition as a Social Process*, administers the advanced writing program at the University of Alabama at Birmingham where he also teaches courses in composition studies, rhetorical theory, discourse analysis, professional writing, and visual communication.

Rhetorical Philosophy and Theory Series

The Rhetorical Philosophy and Theory series aims to extend the subject of rhetoric beyond its traditional and historical bounds and thus to elaborate rhetoric's significance as a metaperspective in provocative ways. Rhetoric has become an epistemology in its own right, one marked by heightened consciousness of the symbolic act as always already contextual and ideological. Otherwise known as the rhetorical turn, this dialectic between rhetoric and philosophy may lead to views transcending the limits of each and thus help us better understand the ethical problems and possibilities of producing theory.

The Rhetorical Philosophy and Theory series seeks quality scholarly works that examine the significance of rhetorical theory in philosophical, historical, cultural, and disciplinary contexts. Such works will typically bring rhetorical theory to bear on the theoretical statements that enfranchise disciplinary paradigms and practices across the human sciences, with emphasis on the fields of rhetoric, composition, philosophy, and critical theory.

Queries and submissions should be directed to David Blakesley, Editor, Rhetorical Philosophy and Theory, Department of English, Purdue University, West Lafayette IN 47907.